EVERYONE CAN WIN

How to Resolve Conflict

EVERYONE CAN WIN

How to Resolve Conflict

HELENA CORNELIUS AND SHOSHANA FAIRE

SIMON & SCHUSTER

AUSTRALIA

Dedicated to
Stella Cornelius, AO, OBE
whose wisdom and compassion
continually inspire us.

EVERYONE CAN WIN

First published in Australasia in 1989 by
Simon & Schuster Australia

20 Barcoo Street, East Roseville, NSW 2069

Reprinted 1989, 1990 (three times), 1991 (three times), 1992,
1993 (twice), 1994 (twice)

A division of Paramount Communications Inc.

National Library of Australia
Cataloguing in Publication data

Cornelius, Helena.
Everyone can win : how to resolve conflict.

ISBN 0 7318 0111 3.

1. Conflict management. 2. Interpersonal
relations. 3. Interpersonal conflict.
I. Faire, Shoshana. II. Title.
302.3

Designed by Jack Jagtenberg
Illustrations by Roger Roberts
Typeset by Midland Typesetters

Printed in Australia by McPherson's Printing Group

CONTENTS

Acknowledgments

First, we would like to thank the thousands of course participants who trialled, polished and expanded each of the skills in the book and then fed the information back to us so that we could improve our program.

We would particularly like to acknowledge our debt to two great teachers for a number of key concepts—Robert Kiyosaki of the Excellerated Learning Institute, and Thomas Crum of Windstar Foundation and Aiki Works.

Many members of The Network contributed their expertise. Particular thanks to Daniel Braham, Gill Goater, Patricia Janssen, Mike Minehan and Kerrie Murray. Rita Spencer has made significant contributions to Chapter 7 on managing other people's unwillingness to resolve and Chapter 11 on conflict creators. Christine James, co-producer of the 12-part audio cassette series *The Resolution of Conflict*, has put together the program notes and group exercises that are cross-referenced in Appendix B.

Thanks also to Dr Greg Tillett of the Conflict Resolution Foundation of Macquarie University and to Jennifer David of the Australian Commercial Disputes Centre for their contributions to the chapter on mediation. Our thanks to Sonya Hall for her untiring wordprocessing through many drafts; and to Stella Cornelius, who at 6.30 each morning, would edit whatever we had written the day before; and to Debbie, Kerry and Martin who tolerated with good grace our interminable discussions on each section. Thanks, too, to Simon & Schuster and two wonderful people: our editor Susan Morris-Yates and Kirsty Melville who held the vision of the finished book.

And, lastly, may we acknowledge you, the reader, for your commitment to find a better way.

Introduction

Everyone Can Win is a new concept of winning that does not infer that someone else is losing. It shows how everyone can gain something from a transaction. The image of victory and defeat is replaced by a partnership in problem solving.

The ideas in this book are commonsense. However, they're not yet very common. People in conflict don't usually pay as much attention to the other person's needs as they do to their own. After you've read the book, we hope you'll speak up for the win/win approach. You'll find many tips for convincing your win/lose opponent that win/win is a better way to play. You'll get more of what you want more of the time—and so will the people around you. Of course, there will be times when you won't *appear* to win, but you'll have turned the situation into an opportunity.

The field of conflict resolution is immense, but as yet has been largely undefined. In 1986, the International Year of Peace, the United Nations Association of Australia founded The Conflict Resolution Network as part of their peace program. Its purpose was to develop, teach, implement and learn the skills of conflict resolution for personal, professional and international effectiveness. In order to have peace in the world the starting place is to handle conflict effectively in our daily lives.

Observing people in conflict and drawing from fields as diverse as management and child rearing, psychology and the martial arts, personal development and critical thinking, The Network carefully constructed a package of key skills. These skills rapidly became useful 'filing drawers' for classifying a wide range of thought and literature on the subject of conflict resolution. They became the substance of the teaching program. Their significance and relevance in improving people's lives became abundantly clear.

The Conflict Resolution Network has taught people in business, government and community organisations. It supports programs introducing the skills in schools and tertiary education (for example, law, town planning, medicine, nursing, social work, psychology and communication studies). The skills have been found particularly relevant to management, unions, 'front counter' staff in any organisation, grievance officers, Aboriginal groups, politicians, environmental and peace groups, and many others who may find themselves in conflict. These are the skills which can help people move from an adversarial approach to one of co-operation. Such an approach is better for business, community action, and personal relationships.

Everyone Can Win presents you with tools not rules. Each chapter introduces one of the 12 'tools' in your 'toolkit'. Just as a tool has many uses, so these skills can be transferred across diverse spheres of activity. The skills you teach a young child are basically the same ones needed by an international diplomat. One morning at 7 o'clock, you'll pull out a 'tool' for a problem in the kitchen, and find yourself needing it again in a difficult business meeting at 11 o'clock. In choosing our examples and stories we reflect this variety of contexts and the transferability of the skills.

What are the tools in this toolkit? Here's a brief run down:

Chapter 1   Win/Win: everyone's needs are respected.

Chapter 2   Creative Response: problems are turned into possibilities.

Chapter 3   Empathy: communication tools build rapport. Hear how it is on the other side. Listen so people will talk.

Chapter 4   Appropriate Assertiveness: attack the problem not the person. Say how it is on your side. Talk so people will listen.

Chapter 5   Co-operative Power: defuse power struggles. Build 'power with' the other person.

Chapter 6   Managing Emotions: fear, anger, hurt and frustration can be handled wisely for effective change.

Chapter 7   Willingness to Resolve: recognise personal issues clouding the picture.

Chapter 8   Mapping the Conflict: chart all the factors involved to build a common vision.

Chapter 9   Designing Options: design creative solutions together.

Chapter 10 Negotiation: effective planning and strategies to reach agreement.

Chapter 11 Mediation: help others to understand each other and build solutions.

Chapter 12 Broadening Perspectives: see the problem in its broader context and in an expanded time frame.

In conflict, one or two of these skills will be particularly relevant in solving the problem. The rest will sit in your toolkit waiting for another context. Use the Conflict Checklist in the Appendices to analyse a problem in detail or to quickly decide which tool is most needed in a given situation. Further information is given in the cross-referenced program notes for the twelve-part audio cassette series *The Resolution of Conflict* (ABC Enterprises, Sydney, 1989). The tapes parallel the chapters in this book. The program notes, with or without the tapes, provide additional support for group work or home study.

As you read *Everyone Can Win,* try to associate the skills with your own experience. The boxed stories may remind you of similar incidents. You'll learn the skills much faster by relating to them, rather than only studying them theoretically.

This is not a book to read once and put away. Keep it handy and reach for it any time you hear, see or feel conflict developing. Pin up somewhere obvious a relevant catchphrase from one of the marginal key points, or run through a chapter summary with someone else. Work with the book until it is part of your life. 'Love thy neighbour' takes skill and practice.

The aim of *Everyone Can Win* is to celebrate conflict, not to squash it. It is designed to help you to get what you want and to see conflict as creative opportunity. Successful conflict resolution releases energy, joy, and a sense of achievement. Homes become self-esteem factories, schools transform into discovery stations, workplaces change into environments of mutual support and growth and the planet can achieve the co-operation of a global community.

Do you want richer relationships? Do you want more things done better? Do you want to have more fun in life? READ ON!

Introducing Conflict

Have you ever slammed the door in rage as you walked out? Have you ever been really hurt by something someone said? Have you ever had a fight with your mother? If the answer's yes to any of these, you've been in conflict.

Have you ever wished you could have dealt with it differently? You've been dealing with conflict all your life one way or another, and you've already developed some skills. You might like to acquire some more. That's what this book is about.

As individuals with different needs, tastes, views and values we are bound to encounter conflict. The issue is how we cope with it.

Conflict can flare up over back fences or national borders; over cleaning up the kitchen or cleaning up the environment. It can involve our most intimate relationships or the briefest interactions. When people cannot tolerate others' moral, cultural, religious or political differences, conflict is inevitable and often costly.

Conflict can open avenues of change and provide challenges. Conflict resolution skills do not guarantee a solution every time, but they can turn conflict into an opportunity for learning more about yourself and others.

First, look at what happens when conflict arises. What do you see happening when a conflict is badly managed or ignored? Consider the following list:

anxiety
withdrawal
procrastination
helplessness
confusion
deterioration
denial
separation
escalation
polarisation

loneliness
suppressed anger
loss of productivity
lassitude
resentment
high blood pressure
stress
tiredness
illness
broken crockery!

In contrast, what do you see happening when conflict is managed skilfully? Consider the second list:

a sense of smooth running	a sense of achievement
comfort	a sense of expansion
fun	teamwork
vitality	change
happiness	growth
openness	expanded relationships
efficiency	peace
feeling of power	relaxation
relief	good health
comradeship	restful sleep

Conflict is an opportunity.

Conflict can be positive or negative, constructive or destructive, depending on what we make of it. Certainly it is rarely static—it can change at any time. We can sometimes alter its course simply by viewing it differently. We can even turn our fights into fun. Transforming conflict this way is an art, though, requiring special skills. The first thing we must learn is that our fights and personal differences are part of life and that it is a mistake to avoid conflict. Life can be less painful if we learn to anticipate a potential conflict and manage it constructively.

Conflict resolution depends greatly on awareness, and there are clues which range from the obvious to the subtle. They are *conflict clues.*

CONFLICT CLUES

Crisis

A crisis is certainly an obvious clue. When someone walks out on a relationship or job, it's plain there has been a conflict which is probably unresolved.

Violence is a sure sign of crisis, as is heated argument where people hurl abuse and become overwhelmed by their feelings. During crises normal behaviour goes out the window. Extreme gestures are contemplated and sometimes carried out.

Tension

Tension is another obvious clue. Your own tension distorts your perception of another person and most of what they do. The relationship becomes weighed down with negative attitudes and fixed opinions. The way you feel about the other person changes significantly for the worse. The whole relationship is a source of

frequent worry. A tense situation is like dry brush just waiting for a spark to set it crackling. When a couple are sitting at their dinner-table and he says, 'Pass the salt', and she snaps back, 'Don't you like my cooking any more?' it is quite likely that something amiss has led to this exchange. Perhaps he'd been late home a few times and she had drawn some conclusions without much evidence to back them—quite possibly it was all a misunderstanding.

Misunderstanding

People often misunderstand each other by making false assumptions about a situation, usually because of unclear communication or lack of rapport. Sometimes misunderstanding arises because the situation raises a touchy issue for someone. Your thoughts are likely to keep returning to the same problem. Perceptions of the problem are distorted.

Incidents

The clue that you are experiencing a conflict incident is usually a minor one. Some minor thing happens that leaves you feeling rather upset or irritated for a while, and then often the problem is forgotten within a few days. In our 'Pass the salt' and 'Don't you like my cooking any more?' example, her tension and misunder-standing may have been preceded by several small incidents, such as his forgetting to phone a couple of times. 'Better not make a fuss,' she'd thought at the time—but these little omissions kept simmering in the back of her mind. In itself an incident is a simple problem, but if it is perceived badly it may escalate.

Discomfort

Discomfort is the intuitive feeling that something is wrong, even though you can't put your finger on it. This is when your intuition deserves respectful attention—in fact, you can welcome it. Ask yourself, 'Is there something I could do *now* about this?' You may soon find yourself on a course of action that would not have occurred to you before. At other times there may be nothing to do except stay alert.

Look for the conflict clues.

If you learn to recognise the clues of discomfort and incidents and deal with them promptly, you can often save a situation from tension, misunderstanding or crisis.

SUMMARY

The first step in the art of resolving conflict is to regard conflict as opportunity and look for the *conflict clues*.

CHAPTER ONE

Win/Win—Opponents or Partners?

The win/win approach to conflict does not come naturally to everyone. It requires skills some of us may not have acquired in our childhood.

As soon as we're in a conflict or see one looming up, we can *choose* our approach. But sometimes we fail to choose and revert to a knee-jerk reaction. We might think our reaction is natural, but many of our 'natural' reactions are actually habits, some of them acquired early in life. If you handle conflict much the same way each time, you have fallen into one of several 'conflict habits'.

WITHDRAWAL

If you physically or emotionally withdraw from a conflict, perhaps from fear of confrontation, you no longer have a say in what happens.

It is wise, however, to withdraw when the conflict is none of your business and your lack of involvement does not affect what's going on. It can even be a helpful response if it draws attention to a neglected crisis.

On the other hand, you might prompt someone to give in too easily, become too demanding, or withdraw too, instead of contributing to a solution. Withdrawal can leave a problem to grow out of proportion. Be careful, too, that your withdrawal does not punish someone. It is often used, consciously or unconsciously, to make someone change their mind.

Do you withdraw to punish?

The reactions listed below are all forms of withdrawal. Think about what happens when you disagree with someone, and see if any apply to you. Do you . . .

- Stop talking?
- Storm off in a huff?
- Retire hurt?
- Become resentful?
- Become depressed?
- Give them the cold shoulder?
- Say cutting things about them later?
- Move to a 'business only' level?
- Stop caring about them?
- Cross them off your list of friends or business associates?

SUPPRESSION

Refusing to acknowledge conflict is the habit we resort to when we need peace at any cost. Suppression is sensible, though, when a confrontation over a slight disagreement puts too much pressure on the relationship, or when people are not ready to hear what you have to say. Sometimes, too, you can preserve a relationship by choosing tact over brutal honesty. Conflicts can even dissolve just because you stay friendly.

'Anything for peace' is dangerous.

Suppressing a serious conflict means you don't talk about its main issues. If you keep silent, the other person does not know all that's going on with you. Even if they sense something is wrong, they can't find out what really is the matter.

In conflict, do you . . .

- Act as if nothing is the matter?
- Plough on regardless?
- Put up with it for the sake of peace?
- Scold yourself afterwards for being so upset?
- Use charm to get your own way?
- Say nothing at the time but scheme later on?
- Bottle up all your bad feelings?

All these strategies are various forms of suppression.

WIN/LOSE

The win/lose habit is often prompted by an unconscious compulsion to protect yourself from the pain of being wrong. Win/lose is a power struggle in which one person comes out on top. It is sometimes necessary, though, for an experienced person in authority (e.g. a boss, a parent, a teacher) to lay down the law for everyone's sake. It is certainly necessary that someone takes over if people need protection from violent or rash behaviour. Win/lose, however, is seldom a long-term answer—the loser may not support a decision they did not take part in, and may even try to sabotage it. Today's loser may refuse to co-operate tomorrow.

Beware the loser.

These are some win/lose tactics. Do you . . .

- Set out to prove the other person wrong?
- Sulk until they change their mind?
- Shout them down?
- Turn physically violent?
- Refuse to take 'no' for an answer?
- Lay down the law?
- Outsmart them?
- Call in allies to back you up?
- Demand that the other person gives in to save the relationship?

COMPROMISE

Compromise employs some negotiation skills so that everyone gains something. It seems fair—'How much for you? How much for me?'—but this can imply that there is not enough for everyone to have everything they'd like. However, dividing things equally is often accepted as the fairest thing to do, and if you can't make a bigger 'pie', at least everyone shares what is available.

Could you get a bigger pie?

The disadvantages of compromise are that one side may inflate its position to appear magnanimous. One person may give in far more than the other. Sometimes neither side may feel much commitment to a plan that falls short of what they want. If the options are not explored thoroughly, a compromise may turn out to be something less than the best solution.

In conflict, do you manage to . . .

- Maintain the friendship?
- Find out what's fair?
- Divide the prize equally?
- Avoid being dictatorial or pulling rank?
- Gain something for yourself?
- Avoid a clash of wills?
- Give in a bit to preserve the relationship?

Withdrawal, suppression, win/lose and *compromise* are the four most common 'conflict habits'. Whenever habit blocks flexibility difficulties arise, especially when we persist in trying to prove our point instead of cooling down, or when we pretend everything's all right when we should work on a compromise. Withdrawal, suppression, win/lose and compromise are all appropriate at certain times, but we need skill and flexibility to use this repertoire to full advantage.

WIN/WIN— EVERYONE WINS

There is one more strategy to add to a good conflict repertoire— the *win/win* approach. It is commonly believed that to have a winner there must also be a loser. This is true of competitive sport, but it's not a hard and fast rule elsewhere in life. In many circumstances, everyone involved can win something. Instead of 'I want to win,

so I'd better not let you win', try: 'I want to win and I want you to win too!' Instead of 'They are bigger and stronger than me, I'd better beat them or give in. It's you or me,' try: 'you *and* me'.

The advantages of a win/win approach are that you discover better solutions; relationships grow better and stronger; when both people win, both people are tied to the solution; if you're going to deal with a person more than once (and even if you are not) it pays dividends to deal fairly with them; and it feels so good you'll want to do it again!

I want to win
and
I want you to win
too.

How Do You Make Win/Win Work?

You are in the kitchen with two people, and they both want the last orange. What would you do? Cut it in half? Toss a coin? Decide who needs it most? When problems confront us we look for solutions—sometimes far too quickly. The win/win approach requires you to find out more about the situation first and explore the options before thinking about the final solution.

Step 1. Find out why they need what they want.
Let's return to the kitchen.

Go back to needs.

    You: 'What do you want the orange for?'
    One person: 'I'm thirsty. I want the juice.'
    You: 'What do you want the orange for?'
    The other person: 'I want to make a cake. I want the rind.'

Step 2. Find out where the differences dovetail.
Our enquiry shows two people wanting the same thing for different reasons. This is not surprising. Individual differences in personality, purpose and interest constantly create a divergence of needs, but you'll notice them only if you go looking for them.

Where do the differences dovetail?

Step 3. What are the options.[1]
Where one person wants the juice and the other wants the rind, the answer is obvious since each one can take what they want from a whole orange. Win/win solutions are sometimes easy. But suppose it isn't so simple and you both want the orange because you are both thirsty? What are the options? Sharing the juice is the obvious compromise. You could also add sugar and water; buy more oranges; find one of you something else to drink.

Design new options.

Step 4. Co-operate.
You can, on your own, go back to needs, see where the differences dovetail and design new options, but it's much more effective if you co-operate. This way you make it clear that you are treating the other person as a partner, not an opponent. When you both agree on the best option, the relationship is at least maintained,

We do it better together.

at best enhanced. You certainly achieve more than you would by going away angry or deprived.

If you cut the orange in half because you are both thirsty, your solution may resemble a compromise or win/lose approach. But if the relationship is maintained or improved then the outcome differs from that of compromise and win/lose. The point of this approach is that though we may not achieve perfect dovetailing, we look together for win/win solutions. We are definitely more likely to find them when we acknowledge and value each others' needs.

Here are some useful guidelines for seeking win/win solutions:
- Define everyone's needs.
- Try to meet everyone's needs.
- Support other people's values as well as your own.
- Try to be objective and separate the problem from personalities.
- Concentrate on fairness, not pressure.
- Look for creative and ingenious solutions.
- Be hard on the problem but soft on the people.[2]

Partners Not Opponents

I want what's fair for all of us.

The win/win approach creates partners, not opponents. It means searching for ways to involve and satisfy everyone. It can build success in business and enrich personal life. Beware the loser if you persist with the win/lose habit. The company that exploits workers can end up with industrial strife; the nation that suppresses an ethnic group often precipitates revolt; the marriage that oppresses one partner can end in irreconcilable discord or collapse.

GILL'S STORY

My two boys (5 and 7) were fighting again! This time it was over who should get to play with Trevor's new toy tractor. I wondered: 'Should I just order Jeremy to give it back to Trevor, or is it time for Trevor to learn to share?' They were getting violent. I would have to arbitrate yet again—if only I could decide who was in the right. Suddenly I saw that neither alternative explored possibilities, and that my answer, whatever it was, might not be the best way to teach them to fix their own fights. It was time to try another way. I said to them both: 'Well, what shall we do about this? What do you each want?' I tried to sound caring, curious and open. Of course, they both wanted a turn with the

tractor but very quickly one child said, 'I don't mind if he has it today as long as I get it tomorrow.' I was amazed how quickly they had produced a new option. What's more, they both agreed to it! I think I had been underestimating them. I liked myself better, too, when I wasn't wielding authority over them—I'd simply got them going in the right direction. Trevor played with his tractor the next day and I watched how they handled it. Would he give it up? Would Jeremy ask for his end of the bargain? Jeremy just said, 'It's my turn today,' and Trevor quite happily handed it over. For once, they didn't squabble about it. Not only had they reached their own solution, they had stuck to it!

Even when trust between the parties is very limited, the win/win approach can work. If there's any doubt that the other person will keep their end of the bargain, you can make the agreement reciprocal. For example, 'I'll do X for you if you do Y for me'; 'I'll drive you to the party if you clean the car'; 'I'll help you draw up those figures for your reports if you sort out these invoice queries'.

Win/win is a successful strategy. You don't have to be an altruist to adopt it because it simply seeks conflict resolution for mutual gain.

Win / win seeks conflict resolution for mutual gain.

Openers

It's good to open the win/win approach with some sort of a conversational headline. 'I want what's fair for all (or both) of us' will often swing things in the right direction. It's very hard for the other person to reject the principle of fairness! Another opener— 'Let's see how we can both have what we want'—proves you're not out to fight. If the other person is hard to budge, you might try 'I'm here to solve problems.' It's very hard to reply: 'Well, I'm not!'

Next, probe below the surface disagreement with questions such as: 'Why does that seem the best solution to you?'; 'What's your real need here?'; 'What values are important to you here?'; and 'Suppose this was fixed?'

Answering these questions makes a dramatic impact on the discussion agenda. You need to have before you the right information for co-operative problem solving. You've also created an opportunity to present your own needs.

WIN/WIN DILEMMAS

You may be thinking that you can't always have a win/win solution. You may have reservations such as the following.

1. What about a friend who never reciprocates favours?
   Try telling them: 'I want us to stay friends and I find that hard to manage when I don't feel I'm getting anything back from you.'

2. What about trading with another business that seems headed for bankruptcy? Should my business provide them with prompt service?
   Try telling them: 'I realise you are in a tight financial situation right now, but my company can't risk not getting paid. I'll have to have cash on delivery. Would it be easier to pay immediately if you had smaller, more frequent deliveries?'

3. Suppose you are in direct competition with others for the same promotion?
   Try to stop worrying about the others and concentrate on

Competition is an opportunity for achievement.

SHOSHANA'S STORY

I went into the store early Saturday morning, all excited. I had come to pick up the new tape deck I had ordered. It was a brand new model and I was really splurging on myself. When I arrived, the salesman greeted me with: 'Yes, it's arrived. But it's the only one I have. I want to keep it in the store for the day for display." I had so badly wanted it for this weekend. A range of possibilities ran through my mind. Faced with this sort of frustration I usually react impulsively instead of <u>carefully choosing the best approach. Having steeped myself in conflict resolution studies recently, here I was at a moment of choice.</u>

I could do any of the following:

- *Insist on my rights—loudly.*
- *Remind him that since he had agreed to sell it to me, he had better honour his agreement straight away.*
- *Try to be nice, let him have it for the day and say I'll come back later, even though it is very inconvenient.*
- *Pretend I don't especially want it for the weekend.*
- *Say 'Forget it—I'll go to another store!'*
- *Start constructing a win/win situation.*

If we could swing it, the last option would certainly leave us both better friends. I stood there wondering how to do it, waiting for possibilities to drop into the silent space. I really didn't want to come back, nor leave without it. I wanted that machine! The man was very nice and I didn't want to be on bad terms with him. Suddenly he said, 'Where do you live?' I told him and he said he passed right by there on his way home—could he bring it to me later in the day?

I thought about it and realised there were advantages in this. I wouldn't have to carry the tape deck and I could do more shopping. I didn't mind waiting a few hours. I just didn't want to be without it for the whole weekend.

This win/win brought further pluses. When the salesman delivered the tape deck he took the time to set it up for me and explain all the features. (I probably would never have read the instructions very carefully.) We had an enjoyable conversation and now I know I can rely on him for good advice. Sometimes I drop by just to say 'hi'.

We both gave a bit. He had to take extra time to drop it off to me, I had to hold off for a few hours. They were concessions we could both live with.

yourself. Competition is always an opportunity for accomplishment, whatever the outcome. Getting the promotion may or may not be a win. The real win is doing your best.

Strengthen your own game rather than worsen your opponent's.

4. What do you do when the opposition (e.g. in business or sport) is bigger, stronger or better?

Try strengthening your own game instead of weakening your opponent's play. The following story from *Zen in the Martial Arts*[3] illustrates the point.

In sparring practice, a martial arts student was being constantly frustrated by a more skilful opponent. He had used his entire repertoire of tricky moves, but each had been readily countered. At the end of the match, thoroughly dejected, he went to his teacher for advice. His teacher, seeing him upset, drew a chalk line on the floor about 2 metres long.

'How can you make this line shorter?' he asked. The student studied the line and made several suggestions, including cutting the line in many pieces. The teacher shook his head and drew a second line, longer than the first.

'Now how does the first line look?'

'Shorter,' the student said.

The teacher nodded. 'It is always better to improve your own line or knowledge than to try and cut your opponent's line.'

5. Suppose you're the parent of a young teenager who has stolen a car.

First, bail them out—they still need your support. Tell them how you feel about it. Outline the penalties you and the law will deal out, and point out how their career could suffer from getting into trouble with the law. Try the win/win approach too. Ask them why they did it and delve below the surface for anything in their life that may have contributed to this extreme behaviour. Maybe there is

SONYA'S STORY

My husband recently decided to become a self-employed contractor and he needed to share my car until the new business got going. It looked as if it could work because I started early and finished early. He agreed to take me to work and collect me.

One afternoon he was about half an hour late. He explained that away—'business comes first'. Then he came forty-five minutes late and the excuse was the same. 'Besides,' he said, 'you probably didn't have anything special or urgent to do then, anyway.' This time I was furious. I felt slighted and undervalued. I had, in fact, planned to take work home to do that afternoon and I lost forty-five minutes' working time. Also, my mother was coming over for dinner. My husband had been held up because a man had been late for an afternoon appointment with him.

'Why couldn't you have explained to him you had a prior commitment?' I asked. 'You could have continued talking after we got home or on another day.' I was very short with him.

'I didn't think I needed to do that. I thought you saw getting my business going as our first priority,' he said.

'And what about my business in the meantime?' I asked. 'I'm supposed to just

understand and wait around like the patient little wife!' Tempers were heated. I felt abused. I knew I had to stick up for my rights. The original car arrangement had been a win/win, but it was rapidly breaking down because he wasn't keeping his end of the bargain.

I felt guilty about saying firmly, 'You can't borrow the car if you can't keep your commitment to collect me on time. I understand your priorities, but I still want my needs met. I've got a life to live too.' He agreed that perhaps he shouldn't always use the car as a matter of course.

The next time he needed the car he was right on time to collect me. The real test of the win/win requirement came on another day when he said he wouldn't borrow the car because he couldn't guarantee he could collect me at the appointed time!

Now that our rules for fair co-operation are clearly laid down, he knows he must collect me on time when he borrows the car.

Sonya had to be very assertive to defend her needs in this disagreement with her husband over priorities. However, it was important to correct the problem. If the arrangement wasn't working for Sonya, as well as for her husband, the relationship was at risk.

something you should or could do to meet their need for excitement, perhaps, or independence. Perhaps they need companionship.

6. What about direct hostility such as theft, murder and terrorism? How should you punish it?

We have to respond forcefully to aggression and law breaking. Police, prisons, armed forces and the law have essential—and difficult—roles in ensuring safety, security and fair play. But how can you pursue the win/win strategy when the other side refuses to co-operate?

Retaliation to international terrorism may discourage further violence for the time being, but solves nothing. It merely creates a short-term stalemate.

If nations would only maintain dialogue. Find out more about the

JOE'S STORY

Joe had just purchased a run-down old factory which he planned to rebuild. He shared his driveway and parking bay with the factory next door. Alongside the other factory, the parking bay was concreted, but Joe's side of it wasn't. In wet weather Joe's side got muddy, so he had made a habit of parking on the concrete. Joe's new building plans included concreting the area, but he couldn't get council approval until Stan, the next-door factory owner, approved the plans. Stan had kept the documents on his desk for months and refused to sign them. Joe was completely frustrated with this unreasonable delay. Every time Joe asked about the documents, Stan became more aggressive. Sometimes Joe would completely lose his temper and attack Stan: 'Why the hell won't you approve my plans? They've been in for five months, now.' Stan would retaliate by calling him a nuisance, troublemaker, migrant, intruder and so on.

One day Joe decided to try the win/win approach. He went to Stan and said, 'I'm wondering if you're not approving my plans because I park where you don't like. Where would you like me to park?' Stan started to get angry again, but Joe said, 'Hey, I'm not getting angry with you. I'm looking for a

solution. I'm willing to do what you want. I'll park somewhere else, except when it rains!'

Joe parked on his side for several days. Then it rained. He rang Stan and said, 'I've parked off the concrete for a while and now it's raining, what do you think I should do? There is mud everywhere on the other side.'

'I dunno,' was the best Stan could come up with.

Joe persisted: 'I've done something for you. I've let you establish that side of the parking bay as yours. But today I need to park on the concrete. I won't ever need to park on it if I can concrete the other side, and I'll do that as soon as I get my new building started. How about approving those plans? You'll be winning if I park out of your area and I'll be winning if I get my building work done. I want to play ball with you, what are you willing to do?'

Stan didn't respond immediately but Joe felt he had improved his bad image. He'd shown Stan he was prepared to co-operate. He was on a better track than the angry attack he had used before. Stan's stubborn stance took a while to break down. Joe was put to the test several more times before Stan finally signed his plans, but his consistent win/win approach helped Stan build trust in him.

problem. We must continue to develop options together to gain even the smallest degree of international understanding and keep working at it. Whatever else you are doing, the win/win approach has a universal application.

Prison and deprivation of liberty is a punishment often required by law. Offenders play win/lose and society needs to redress the balance. But punishment alone doesn't do much to re-educate a criminal. Crime is sometimes a person's reaction to many things that have gone wrong in their life. One of the most basic of these is a very low sense of self-esteem. Some criminals have poor communication skills and many don't know any better way to get what they want. Other factors may be lack of an adequate education and the skills to earn an honest living, or being the victims of unemployment. Many have known nothing but violence and lack of consideration all their life.

A law breaker deserves society's punishment, but also needs society's help. One day the sentence is over, we open the prison door and they walk out, free. Whom are we releasing? A bitter, inadequate piece of flotsam who knows how to survive only through crime or violence? Or is this a person with a new start, who has enough sense of self-worth not to sink into crime? Has the offender now developed skills for work and personal friendship, become employable and received (perhaps for the first time) some respect? A prison system that managed such a transformation would certainly make a win for society as well as for the prisoner.

7. What about someone who won't co-operate?

The task is always to continue the win/win approach, to show others the value and benefits of co-operation. Don't give up on win/win. Moving to a win/lose approach won't teach co-operation. Your best chance of changing them is to continue offering an alternative.

Don't give up on win/win.

If a family member won't co-operate, don't freeze them out of your affections. Keep offering support even if the other person remains hostile. Don't condone bad conduct, just be clear about how much support you are willing to give them.

The win/win approach is sometimes a long process which might need perseverance. Of course, the end result is important, but it is during the process of reaching that result that the real benefits— better options, mutual respect, commitment and goodwill—appear.

SUMMARY

Withdrawal, suppression, win/lose, compromise and win/win are all conflict strategies you can call on. The most successful is the win/win strategy, and these are the four steps to follow:

1. Find out why they need what they want.
2. Find out where differences dovetail.
3. Design new options where everyone gets more of what they need.
4. Do it together. Make it clear you're partners, not opponents.

Where both people win, both are committed to the solution because it suits them and they have been involved during the entire process. The best thing about win/win is that it is a completely ethical approach that works.

NOTES

1. For more on developing options, see Chapter 7: Designing Options.
2. See Roger Fisher and William Ury, *Getting to Yes* (UK: Arrow, 1981).
3. Joe Hyams, *Zen in the Martial Arts* (US: Bantam Books, 1979), p. 36.

CHAPTER TWO

Creative Response— Problems or Challenges?

The creative response to conflict is about turning problems into opportunities. It means extracting the best from a situation.

How many of the following are familiar to you?

- A situation looks hopeless and has really got you down.
- You just had a business deal go sour.
- You just missed out on something you really wanted.
- Something you did upset somebody.
- You just made a giant boo-boo.
- You thought you'd met the man or woman of your dreams and they went off with your best friend.

Step 1: Reaction or Response

When a situation gets you down, the skill of 'creative response' is just the one you need. By *react* we mean here *behave impulsively,* especially when you feel you can't control your behaviour or feel forced into behaving a certain way. Someone or something else is seen as the cause of your reaction. By *respond* we mean here *behave thoughtfully* so that you feel in command and are not swept away.

When someone around us is in a bad mood or doesn't want to do what we want, we can *react* in a number of ways:

Will you react or respond?

- We can withdraw.
- We can say how they ought to behave.
- We can become cranky ourselves.
- We can work out some way of getting back at them.

On the other hand we can *respond* to the situation by exploring its possibilities. What would it take to turn it around in some way?

JUSTIN'S STORY

I bumped into an old acquaintance in a coffee lounge, made the mistake of asking how he was, and found myself bombarded with his latest philosophy on pollution.

I was so irritated I just wanted to walk away. All I could think was: 'The guy's a nut' . . . 'what a neurotic twit' . . . 'how could anyone carry on like that?'

Then I stopped this chatter in my mind and thought: 'Ah, conflict. What's a creative response here? OK, this is another human being. I don't really like his ideas but let me hear what the world is like for him.'

I replaced 'nut' and 'twit' thoughts with some open questions to him: 'What would you like to see happen in regard to

pollution?' His ideas on the matter turned out to be quite fascinating! I asked him if he was thinking of moving away from the city. He said that he wanted to, but his family were not at all willing and this was causing him a lot of conflict and confusion. He seemed to relax a bit after he said that and seemed pleased that I had cared to ask and listen.

Somehow I felt a bit different toward him and felt better about myself because of the way I had treated him. As we parted company he smiled warmly. Usually after seeing him I have to shake him off me. This time I felt a lot better.

Step 2: Acknowledge the Situation for What It Is

This doesn't mean 'like' it or even 'want' it—just *accept* how it is right now. Judgment can wipe out your acknowledgment. While you're fighting something, or criticising it, you are not accepting it as it is. You'll know when you've really acknowledged the situation. It might come with a sigh. It comes with some talking to yourself such as: 'Oh well, that's how it is. Might as well stop fighting that fact and start to look toward where I can go from here.'

First, start with where you are right now.

Acknowledge the situation as it is.

It's usually easier to recognise opportunities from this basis. Once you accept the problem, it is more manageable. If someone is in a bad mood, the fastest way to change that is to accept it.

Perfection Yardstick

How much of your time and thoughts are spent focusing on how things ought to be instead of how things are? Do you have some preconceived ideas of how things should be? How people should behave? What ought to happen? Are you constantly deciding what is polite or appropriate? What is efficient, and correct? How people ought to treat you? How you ought to treat them?

Are you sure you're right?

How often do you think: 'She shouldn't speak to me like this'; 'He should do his work better'; 'She shouldn't smile at strangers'; 'He shouldn't tell me he's done something when he hasn't'; 'She shouldn't smell like that'? We're constantly measuring up others and finding them wanting. There is a joke about a mythical philosopher/ sage, Oosez, who responds to judgments with the comment 'Oo sez?' ('Who says?'). You can quote him any time!

What about ourselves? How often do you use this 'perfection yardstick' on yourself? 'If I'm not going to get this right, I'd better not even try'; 'I'm frightened they won't like me when I speak in public'; 'Is my hair looking right?'; 'Am I wearing the right clothes?'; 'Did I do all I should have done today?'; 'I ate too much'; 'I'm no good at . . .' Add some more of your own.

Step 3: *What Can You Learn From the Situation*

As long as we measure the world (including ourselves) with a perfection yardstick, we will be thinking thoughts like these: 'Did I/they get it right?'; 'Did I/they get it wrong?'; 'It was (or wasn't) good enough'; 'I'd better not try this, I might fail'; 'I didn't do it well enough last time so I'd better not do it again'; or 'They weren't nice enough (or good enough) so I won't ask them again'.

How frustrating, if you can't think or move without snatching up the perfection yardstick! Change your baseline. Look at what the situation is and then at what might be. Discover!

Perfection or discovery?

Change your thinking to something like this: 'How they did that is interesting. What can I learn from it?'; 'If I try this I might learn something'; 'How can I make it better next time?'; 'What will stop him complaining to me all the time?'; 'What else can I try to get the kids to help with the washing up?'; 'What are we freed up to do, now that the $9 million order has been cancelled?'

And life becomes fascinating!

It's important to note that the creative response does not gloss over difficulties. Saying everything is fine when it isn't is like coating a rotten apple with toffee. That is not what the creative response is about. You can't pretend that a mistake doesn't need correcting or that you did a good job when you've done a bad one. Nor should you pretend to enjoy listening to someone complain or act as if you don't mind if you don't get help when you need it. You know you *must* rethink and regroup if an important contract is cancelled. With a creative response, you acknowledge how you feel about each of these situations and then turn it into a learning experience. You transform *frustration* into *fascination.* Try 'Ah, how fascinating!' next time you're grinding your teeth in irritation.

When the photostat machine has just broken down again, or a client has just abused you, or the kids have just tramped mud right through the house, what else is there to do but learn from the problem? You could throw a tantrum or cry. Indeed, you may need to let off steam. And then what? Analyse how to prevent it happening again, or find out what is still possible. This is the creative response that will head you back in the right direction.

The Fall is as Interesting as the Next Step

Children learning to walk often simply get up and try again after falling. Children don't judge themselves about whether they are doing something rightly or wrongly. To the young child, a fall can be as interesting as the next step because everything is part of the great experiment. It's only a matter of putting one foot in front of the other. Yet, as adults, we tend to lose this innocent spirit of enquiry. Instead of having a 'right foot, left foot' attitude, self-judgment intervenes and every step in life becomes one of 'right foot, wrong foot'.

What about mistakes? Children who are continually protected from making mistakes can grow up dependent and overly cautious. Bosses who are overly critical of errors often get 'yes-people' to serve in their organisations. A president with too tight a control can trigger a revolution.

What can you learn from the situation?

This doesn't mean you don't point out or correct errors. It means the error should be regarded as a splendid opportunity for learning. You can focus on win/lose or focus on learning. If you focus on learning, losing transforms into a learning opportunity. Life doesn't

---

There is a story about the IBM Company in the US. One middle executive there made a tactical error that cost the company $9 million. The following week the executive was called into the chairman's office. He was sure he was about to be fired. But the chairman started discussing plans for a huge new project he wanted the executive to direct. After a certain point the executive, squirming in his seat, had to interrupt the chairman's train of thought.

'Excuse me, sir. You know, I'm amazed. Last week I cost us $9 million. How come you're putting me in charge of this new project and not firing me?'

The chairman smiled. 'Fire you? Young man, I've just invested $9 million in your education. You're now one of my most valuable assets.'

Here was a chairman who valued above all else the willingness to risk and learn. He knew it was an essential ingredient in any successful executive.

• • •

Thomas Edison 'failed' over 10,000 times before producing a working light bulb. When asked how he could persist after 9,999 failures, he replied simply: 'I did not fail 9,999 times. I succeeded 9,999 times in learning how not to make a light bulb.'

have to be about winning or losing—it can be about winning and learning. When you fall down you have to pick yourself up and note where the pothole was, so you can walk around it the next time.

Learning involves choosing to see things as an interesting experiment, and it makes it much easier to admit when you are wrong. It takes courage, too, to call a halt to a project that's not working out, particularly if it means admitting to a mistake. If your self-esteem depends on being right, it will seem as if you are in big trouble when you are not. Consciously and unconsciously we defend our self-image in the face of our errors. We will even find it hard to recognise our errors if too much depends on being right.

The compulsion to be always right stifles initiative. An organisation which tolerates errors and allows a reasonable amount of risk-taking for the purpose of learning attracts a dynamic staff.

Allow mistakes some room.

Step 4: Turn Conflict Into Opportunity

Recreate the situation. Having chosen to respond rather than react, having accepted it for what it is and having found the lesson, it is time to discover what opportunities the situation offers. Can we turn sour milk into yoghurt? Lemons into lemonade? The challenge is to adopt a creative response in the face of everything.

Creative response calls for a shift in perspective. How can you improve on the status quo? How can you use the problem to build something better than you had before? Can you turn the problem into a doorway for new understanding?

Ah, conflict! What an opportunity.

- You will need to set sail for the positive. *Affirmations* make great navigating devices.
- You need to root out negative attitudes underlying casual remarks. Watch how you use *language* to talk about the problem.
- Redirect your energy to connect with rather than withdraw from the other person, to *greet* rather than reject the problem.

Affirmations

Have you ever told yourself how you want things to turn out? 'It's going to be just fine'; 'It will all work out'. This is an affirmation. Affirmations rely on the assumption that you determine how something will turn out by how you think about it.

If you have to attend your spouse's office party and you decide it will be awful, it probably will be. Decide to make the best of it and you'll find ways to have a good time. Your attitude directs your actions to help make things come out well—another opportunity for turning frustration into fascination!

Example (a): You're worried about a new idea you're trying to

push through at work. Is it really such a good one? Will others block it? Try: 'This project will have everything that it needs to be a great success'. Whenever you think about it and particularly when you start worrying about it say the affirmation to yourself, or write it down and leave your note somewhere prominent.

Example (b): You should have been at an important appointment at 11 a.m. sharp. At 10.50 a.m. you are still twenty minutes' drive away and your usual response might be to try to put your foot down hard on the accelerator. You try an affirmation instead: 'I will be in perfect time'. You don't know what will make it perfect. Perhaps the person you're meeting gets an important telephone call and is relieved that you are late, or perhaps they, too, have a problem reaching the office on time. Maybe you'll get every green light and a totally clear run. You are open to any and every possibility. Thoughts can be powerful enough to change events you apparently have no control over. At the least, such an affirmation would help you arrive in a better frame of mind.

Example (c): You are facing the end of a relationship. So far you haven't been able to reconcile your differences. You're meeting tonight to sort it out or finish it. Whichever way it goes, you want to see the outcome as for the best. As you cope with the butterflies in your stomach, you say to yourself: 'The greatest good will emerge from *this.*'

Language

Just as positive affirmations can affect the outcome, so can any subconscious negative affirmations. They pop up in chance remarks, and in statements of helplessness and hopelessness such as: 'I'll never be able to tell him'; 'She won't listen'; 'It's all hopeless'; 'It's useless trying to do anything'; 'I'll never get through all this work'; 'I can't play the piano'.

Such attitudes can close doors in our lives. Our casual and unconsidered remarks are all affirmations busy moulding the way things are. Problems shift rapidly if we are prepared to correct, deliberately, the way we think and speak. Try these: 'I don't know how to tell him at the moment'; 'She doesn't seem to listen'; 'It seems hopeless right now'; 'I haven't yet figured out what would help'; 'I need a plan to help me get through all this work'; 'I haven't learned to play the piano yet'.

Open doors, don't close them. Who knows what life might bring if you let it! You needn't deny the difficulty you presently face, but you can invite its potential for change. Cynicism, negativity and hopelessness can seem like the only options when you're already caught up in their dark clutches and the world seems stacked against you. But your negativity may be dominating the picture. Change your attitudes and the world might shift too.

As you think, so it becomes.

Greet the Problem

Have you ever sailed through a perfectly lovely day and then met someone in a foul, black mood? What do you do? Quietly resent them for spoiling your day? Act a bit cool and distant and, by the by, happen to notice you've stopped whistling? Do you feel yourself deflating a bit, especially if they come through with any sort of attack? Your coolness and distance probably affects them. Then they feel a bit worse! You notice it, and become a bit colder and more distant. The other person feels even worse, sure now that you don't understand or care about them at all. You are now part of their problem. They're shutting down and you're not looking so good yourself! Before you know where you are, the relationship is literally ended.

What's happening? Both people are withdrawing their energy. When we are well, happy and in touch with other people we are surrounded by energy that's alive, bright, and springy. Our vitality is obvious. Our energy goes out beyond our body to embrace whatever situation we're involved in. There is considerable scientific support for the theory that a measurable high-frequency energy charge emits from all living objects. Some of the most interesting data comes from a form of photography called Kirlian photography. Using high voltages, this method magnifies a person's energy enough to photograph distinct light patterns which vary according to a person's health and mood.

When we react to a situation we don't like, we feel deflated, flat, or slow. This is because we've withdrawn our emotional and physical energy so that we feel separate, even distant from the other person. We certainly know the result of energy contracting. We know when we feel depressed, irritated, 'off the air', for example. But we regard this as something *done to us.*

Because we are normally quite unconscious about these energy changes, we don't recognise them when they happen. We're a light with a dimmer switch control that we can't reach, and it's as if the other person has just turned us down. Most of us don't control what our energy does—but, in fact, we can.

What are the signs, what small physical or internal changes happen when you contract? Think of a food you really hate. Imagine someone is forcing you to eat it right now. What physical sensations happen in your mouth and body as you mentally reject the distasteful food?

Imagine yourself talking to someone you love spending time with. Now imagine that someone you dislike walks into the room and interrupts your conversation. Can you feel your energy contracting? What sensations do you feel as you disguise your irritation? You can redirect your energy more positively once you recognise the signs and take conscious control.

What you can do is to expand instead of contract. Grasp the dimmer switch and turn it up. Brighten up, connect, expand energetically to meet the situation. Do it whenever you notice the signs of your energy withdrawing and it would be better to hang on in there. Try expanding whenever you are in a meeting that's full of hostility and you want to turn it around. Do it when you feel alienated. Do it just before you give a public talk. Do it when it's a great day and you want to enjoy it and be touched by it even more.

Will you connect or contract?

A psychic might see you take charge of your energy. Anyone near you can sense the difference. How you will respond depends on the circumstances. You may sail on, just leaving someone to their bad mood that day and not reacting too much, or you might say something sympathetic, offer to help, or inject some humour into the situation. Direct your energy so that you connect with the situation, stay open to the person and expand rather than contract.

This expansion is important. In effect, you beam out your energy. Mousse, the hair-setting product, fills with thousands of tiny air bubbles when it emerges from its aerosol can, expanding till it occupies much more space than its original volume. This is how you can enfold a difficult person or situation with your expanding energy. Mousse them!

Go out to meet the conflict, not like an army tank with the hatches battened down, but deliberately greeting it as a friend. Expand your energy to embrace and welcome the situation. That's the essence of regarding conflict as opportunity. You're now steering in the right direction, you've tidied up your negative thinking, you've used your energy to connect. You've created a doorway. Now step through and take the opportunity to make things better.

KAREN'S STORY

Creative response concerns changing things moment by moment. I was rushing to catch a plane, a little late as usual and with a bag just a little overweight. The man behind the counter didn't look at all receptive. I feared my lateness and overweight bag would be the last straw in his harassing day. I wanted to turn around and go away, but there were no other free counters. 'Oh no!' I shrank inside, feeling it was all too much. Then, 'Ah yes, how can I make this OK, respond or react?' I 'moussed' him from afar and brightened my own energy.

'It could be worse,' I suggested to him. 'I
could have six heavy bags and five screaming kids.' My comment at least scored a half-smile! He informed me there were no more window seats (I had requested one) and I responded with, 'Gosh, it's hard to complain when I'm the one who was late!' I think he was beginning to appreciate that I wasn't taking it out on him. The smile extended a little more. Creative response was working. He didn't charge me for my overweight bag. I thanked him and wished him a good day and rushed off to catch the plane. I'd made the best of a difficult situation.

SUMMARY

Creative response is all about turning problems into challenges. The four steps are:

1. Will you *react* or *respond*? Choose to respond, to take charge and steer.
2. Acknowledge the situation for what it is. Let go of the demand to be right and perfect all the time and to want others perfect too. But don't let go of your desire for change.
3. What can you learn from this? Open up to what might be. Enquire, discover, be fascinated with mistakes as well as successes. See problems as part of a great experiment.
4. 'Ah conflict, what an opportunity!' Diffuse the conflict by using affirmations, changing negative language and redirecting your energy to greet rather than reject a problem. Do something helpful. You've looked for a doorway, now walk through it.

ADDITIONAL READING

Thomas F. Crum, *The Magic of Conflict* (New York: Simon & Schuster, 1987)

Shakti Gawain, *Creative Visualisation* (California: Bantam, 1978)

Catherine Ponder, *The Dynamic Law of Prosperity* (New Jersey: Prentice-Hall, 1952)

CHAPTER THREE

Empathy— Opening up or Closing Communication

In this chapter we will look at what gets in the way of communication, how we can invite a negative reaction inadvertently, and what we can do to open up communication so we can understand the other person better.

WHAT COOLS COMMUNICATION?

Have you ever been in the middle of telling someone about a problem only to be interrupted with 'You think that's bad? Let me tell you about the time when I . . .'? and they redirect the conversation onto themselves so that you're left feeling ignored and unheard.

Have you ever told someone how angry someone else made you only to hear: 'You're stupid to feel like that'. How do you feel then? Have you ever snapped back 'What would you know!' and walked off? And what about: 'There's nothing to be upset about'? Where does that leave you with your upset? Nowhere, certainly, with that particular person.

It's really quite easy to close off or cool conversation. Consciously and unconsciously we do it all the time. If we really don't want to pursue the matter, that's OK, but often that is not our intention.

We may be cooling off conversations unintentionally due to bad

Does the movie in your head match the play on stage?

habits—that is, ways of reacting we've learned without considering alternatives.

Perhaps, for instance, we are preoccupied with what's happened, with the choreography of our action plan, and with rehearsals of what we are going to say next. Sometimes there's a whole movie going on inside our heads and it's so absorbing we are not tuned in to the other person at all. Another reason for poor communication may lie with our unsureness about coping with someone else, particularly if they are angry or upset. Therefore, you might decide to say nothing, or you might find you've put your foot in it.

There are common 'communication killers' we regularly inflict on each other. We also unconsciously fall into our own variations. Take a few minutes now to answer the questions in the blank columns below. Which communication killers do you use on others? Which ones are used on you? By whom? Consider colleagues, family and friends.

COMMUNICATION KILLERS

Communication killer	Example	Who does it?	
		Self	Others
THREATS (Produces fear, submission, resentment, hostility)	'If you're not able to get to work on time we'll have to review your job here.'; 'Do it or else.'		
ORDERS (Using power over another)	'I'll see you immediately in my office.'; 'Don't ask me why, just do it because I said so.'		
CRITICISM (Put-downs)	'You don't work hard enough.'; 'You're always complaining.'		
NAME-CALLING ('Branding' the other person)	'Only an idiot would say that.'; 'You stupid fool.'; 'What can you expect from a bureaucrat?'		
'SHOULDING' OR 'OUGHTING'	'You should be more responsible.'; 'You ought to face facts.'; 'You shouldn't be so angry.'		

Communication killer	Example	Who does it? Self	Others
WITHHOLDING RELEVANT INFORMATION (With a trap at the end)	'You'll love this project' (not saying how much is involved).		
INTERROGATION	'How many hours did this take you?'; 'How much did this cost?'; 'Why are you so late?'; 'What are you doing?'		
PRAISING TO MANIPULATE	'You're so good at report writing, will you do this one for me?'		
DIAGNOSING MOTIVES	'You're very possessive.'; 'You've always had a problem with motivation.'		
UNTIMELY ADVICE (When the person just wants to be heard)	'If you'd just straighten up your desk, you would not be in this panic.'; 'Why didn't you do it this way?'; 'Just ignore them.'		
PERSUADING WITH LOGIC	'There's nothing to be upset about. It's all quite reasonable.'		
REFUSING TO ADDRESS THE ISSUE	'There's nothing to discuss. I can't see any problems.'		
CHANGING THE TOPIC	'That's interesting . . . I saw a funny movie last night.'		
TOPPING	'I had a dreadful car accident last week . . .' 'You should have seen *mine.*'		
REASSURANCE BY NEGATION	'Don't be nervous.'; 'Don't worry, it will work out.'; 'You'll be fine,'; 'You look terrific.'		

The response you get to your comment matters. Although somewhat doubtful, even these communication patterns can work if the context and tone of voice support the person. People communicate on many layers. The words themselves form only one level. From words and tone· of voice, people constantly interpret (and sometimes misinterpret) data on their relationship with you. If the final result is that they feel you don't respect them, then your communication has not been effective, no matter what your good intentions were. You are responsible for more than the message you give; you are responsible for the communication process and for the message they receive.

Communication killers like those in the table above are common conversational forms which easily persuade people that basic relationship needs are not being met. The message received may not be what was meant. A better choice of words would be wise,

but won't help much if your underlying attitude to the other person is the real stumbling-block.

If your relationships are to work well, your communication must convey to other people that you . . .

- respect them as equals and won't dominate them;
- respect their right to their own opinions and won't manipulate them into seeing it your way[1];
- respect and value their decisions and won't undermine them;
- respect their values and experience.

Empathy blocks:
Domination
Manipulation
Disempowerment
Denial.

Examine your communication style when you feel cut off or blocked out. Ask them what you did that didn't work for them. What did they do that didn't work for you? You can always refine your own skills. How often do you do the very things that irritate you when they're done to you? Finally, if someone else's communication

*Your real
communication is
the response you
get.*

patterns aren't working for you, you may want to find ways to fix the problem. Your objective will be to help them get a better response from you. You might start off with something like this: 'When I receive blunt memos like this one . . .' or 'When you said . . . I felt really put off, and I don't think that's what you intended. There are other ways of making your point that would work better for me.' (See Chapter 4, Appropriate Assertiveness.)

We often shut out someone completely when we have only one or two specific difficulties with them. When the shutters close, empathy is lost and resolving conflict under these circumstances is an uphill battle.

What else closes the shutters? If we meet indifference or dislike, we are likely to protect our tender feelings by shutting down. There are bound to be times when your ideas, wishes, beliefs or actions are challenged—how personally do you take it? You'll be a lot easier to get along with if you can cope with criticism. You don't have to be right all the time to be a worthwhile person!

When a relationship lacks empathy, you can struggle on with it as it is, drop the relationship, or do something about fixing it. Of course, it would be much simpler if the other person fixed it ('after all, it's their fault!'). It would be great if life were about other people changing so you could feel better. But it isn't! The only changes you can control completely are your own.

You won't want to fix every empathy breakdown. But when you can't avoid the person, or you lose out because of the failure of the relationship, it can be worthwhile trying to re-establish rapport.

What makes it worthwhile to improve empathy? Think of three people you have problems with. Find one benefit to you in establishing a better relationship with each of them. It will probably

JENNY'S STORY

There may be times when you don't *want* a relationship to continue.

My father-in-law is an alcoholic. His drinking causes tremendous problems for all of us. He is often aggressive, and when he's not he's filled with self-pity. One day, about a year ago, he came over to our house for a visit. He was drunk and rude and argumentative in front of the children, and I wondered why we let him into the house. We had a huge argument about his drinking and he left, highly offended.

He has not spoken to me since. Of course I've thought about it a lot, but I've chosen not to repair the breach because it means that he doesn't come round any more and I don't have to protect the children from one of his drunken binges.

Because I've made a conscious choice about it, I actually don't feel resentment toward him anymore. I think I've forgiven him for how he is, but I know that I have to acknowledge that his behaviour makes a relationship impossible.

require an effort from you to establish or re-establish a good relationship with them. How will you achieve this?

WHAT WARMS COMMUNICATION?

What makes communication work well? It is *empathy*—the flow between two people whereby each can understand the other's feelings and motives. This link and openness between them is also called *rapport*. To get a sense of this, consider three people you feel open to, and note one quality for each person that helps the empathy flow between you.

You may think of 'friendliness'; 'we have things in common'; 'they'll listen to my problems and tell me about theirs'; 'they don't put me down'; and 'they understand me'. Many of the following characteristics of good empathic relationships will probably also apply.

Empathy Openers

If you have a difficult relationship you may decide to put some effort into sorting it out. One of the ways in which people mistakenly try to do this is by entangling the relationship with the problem. They try to buy a good relationship by giving in. A common approach is 'anything for peace'. For example, a mother might try to bribe a child into good behaviour with junk food. 'Anything for peace' can be a dangerous attitude—it can give the other person too much power. Find other ways to build empathy. There are some tried and true methods you can use:

Work on the relationship separately from the problem.

1. Find a conversation topic you could open up with them. Try a subject totally at a tangent to the problems you are having. What are the other person's interests? When do they most come alive? What excites them? Ask them all about it. A good chat can be a great empathy opener.

Small talk can do a lot in empathy building, however trivial the topic. Any topic will do—the weather; a TV show; music; the football; food; the jumper bought last week; even the relative value of plastic versus metal garbage bins.

The topic is not the real point. You are establishing a flow, tuning in to each other, listening to the music of each other's voices. It's not just the words—there's more to small talk than meets the ear.

2. Sharing an activity can build bridges between you. At work it might be going out together to check out a new piece of equipment; brainstorming a complex project together; or having a working bee on the filing.

I respect them

They value my opinions

We can have fun together

I don't have to wear a mask or be very formal with them

They'll forgive me if I get it all wrong sometimes

They wouldn't ignore me on purpose

I don't have to be perfect around them

I feel open to them

They respect me

EMPATHY IS WHEN

They listen

They don't always have to be perfect around me

They trust me

We like each other

They ask my advice

They tell me things that matter to them

We talk

I see their point of view even though I might not always agree with it

We feel comfortable with each other

I forgive them if they get it all wrong sometimes

They care about me and about what I think

At home, try a board game, going bicycling together, or going to the pictures together.

An activity which gives you something to talk about can help enormously.

3. Choose an appropriate location if you're setting the scene for a real heart-to-heart. You can start a good conversation when driving somewhere together. You have a captive audience and no eye contact in a car, and you can sometimes achieve a similar result while you're both occupied doing the washing up. Sometimes it's worth taking someone to a public place like a coffee-shop, where neither of you is likely to yell or scream.

4. Watch your timing. Don't try for a 'deep and meaningful' conversation when the other person is too rushed or stressed to concentrate.

Empathy With Difficult Parents

Empathy breakdowns with parents are a special case. Some parent-child relationships are disastrous. There's something about parents that can bring out the worst in some of us, perhaps because we're hypersensitised to them and react more emotionally to them than to anyone else. It's not surprising, therefore, that many people are very remote to at least one of their parents. It's sometimes easier to maintain one's distance than to let them constantly interfere.

MARY'S STORY

My father has spent my whole life putting me down. There was a lot of anger and pain in my relationship with him. I realised that it was limiting my whole life but it wasn't easy for me to let go of my feelings of alienation. It probably didn't make any difference to him but I needed to free myself of my own bitterness. First I had to allow myself to fully experience regret—I grieved for what might have been possible in our father-daughter relationship. After that I could accept what positive aspects the relationship offered. We're getting along better than we have ever done; it's not terrific, but it's something.

An advantage of being an adult is that you don't have to take your parents' advice when it doesn't suit you. Unfortunately, if you shut out that parent completely, you may also cut off a basic source of support. It's also a shame when a parent's nurturing is ignored; even if it is expressed badly, the intention may well be loving and concerned.

The aim is to recognise this love as a strength and blessing without engaging in the dramas. The key will probably lie in conversation topics on non-sensitive issues. Think of a tea-strainer. It lets the tea through into the cup but holds back the unwanted tea-leaves.

In these fundamentally nurturing relationships, we can let through whatever level of caring the parent is capable of and use 'tea-strainer' assertiveness to keep the rest at bay.

ROBERT'S STORY

My mother would ring me up to ten times a day, and I'd had enough. I decided that to survive her I needed to disconnect from her as 'mother' since she played this role in a totally smothering fashion. I could cope with her as a friend, which is a role she understands. As a friend she's not nearly as demanding. I made some very clear statements to her about it—I had to get her off my back. A different and much more acceptable relationship has become possible between us now that I've disconnected from her smothering. Now I can really accept her love. She's still being a smother-mother with my brother and sister. They can't understand why she and I get on so well now. I've worked hard to carve out an acceptable relationship with her.

Conscious effort to improve the empathy pays off when the time comes to resolving the differences between you. There may also be some highly sensitive issue that you must agree not to discuss.

People won't hear what you say until they know you care.

Trying to establish a win-win approach when the basic relationship is in a bad way can be extremely difficult. The other person is unlikely to listen to your point of view. You want them to open up to you, but they won't hear you until they know you care about them. So start on that to create the flow.

People usually feel positive when they feel they've been heard and understood. If you want them to hear *you*, then first you need to hear *them*. Empathy grows when communication is opened up so that we can each listen to how it is on the other side.

ACTIVE LISTENING

Good listening is a basic conflict resolution skill. It's easiest to learn by example, but surprisingly few people practise good listening skills. Once you do, others around you might pick up the habit. When you listen closely you drop the normal give and take of conversation for a while. It's a significant shift—like changing gears in a car, and this listening mode is often called *active listening*.

Are you really listening or just awaiting your turn to speak?

Active listening means tuning out your own point of view for a while and tuning in to the other person.

Some Helpful Hints for Active Listening

- Don't talk about yourself.
- Don't change topics.
- Don't advise, diagnose, reassure, encourage, criticise, or bait.

- Don't think ahead about what you will say.
- Don't ignore or deny the other's feelings. Assess how they are feeling from what they are *not* saying as well as what they are! Watch non-verbal communication, e.g., do they have tears in their eyes? Are their body movements agitated?
- Don't pretend you have understood their meaning if you haven't.

- Enquire about their needs, concerns, anxieties and difficulties. Ask questions that encourage them to open up, such as: 'How do you see it all?'
- Confirm that you understand them. Paraphrase the main point you think they are making with: 'Are you saying what you want is . . . ?', 'Are you saying that you don't think you can handle so much pressure?' or 'You feel really angry?'[2]

In conflict situations, there are three distinct uses for active listening skills: information, affirmation and inflammation.

Information—Check the Facts

When you need to give or receive a clear picture or instruction, the communication concerns information. Have you ever arrived somewhere and discovered you were lacking a vital piece of information, or you didn't know what to do next?

Check the facts.

To give a clear picture, the speaker should aim to get across what is wanted. To receive a clear picture, the listener should aim to get all the details, check the facts and ferret out significant information that the speaker is saying or forgetting to say.

HELENA'S STORY

Some time ago I hired Ralph, a consultant, for what I thought would be a couple of days. He was with us as an apprentice Conflict Resolution teacher. His own company wanted him to run a CR course for them and he needed more training for it. I was looking for opportunities to involve him. I thought it would be reasonable for his company to pay his normal wage for two days while he assisted us with a workshop. It suited us very well to have him there, as his background was engineering and this workshop was for a large group of engineers. The workshop formed part of a strenuous two-week assignment we had taken on for a large organisation. Ralph agreed it was a splendid opportunity for in-depth training and went off to his boss to negotiate paid leave. He didn't do well. While I was out one afternoon he left a phone message saying, 'My company won't pay. Can you pay me?' Was he such a bad negotiator that he couldn't get two days paid for doing something of immediate benefit to his company? We could pay him something, but

it didn't sit well with me, even though our trainer really needed his support.

I phoned him back, irritated. I launched right in with: 'Well, the best I can offer you is . . .' Suddenly I stopped myself. It didn't seem fair! Why wouldn't his company pay two days of his wages for his training? I shifted gears. I went fishing for the facts. Casting a wide net, I said: 'Tell me about the problem.' In the next few minutes it emerged that he'd asked for two weeks off, not two days. He thought it would be good for him to assist on the whole project, not just the two-day workshop. Then, of course, I understood why his boss wouldn't pay him for so much time off. We went back to the two-day plan. He talked again with his boss and had no trouble getting a 'yes' for the more modest proposal.

I'd saved the remains of my budget for other things and my gearshift to 'information mode' had rapidly cleared up our misunderstanding and prevented bad feelings.

KATHERINE AND JOHN'S STORY

Katherine and John had been out together several times and their relationship was starting to move into a deeper level. Katherine was discovering for the first time what it was like to trust someone else, be honest about her feelings and reveal her secrets. She felt very close to John. Yet something was getting in the way.

John had children from a previous marriage and she found herself growing angry about the many gifts he bought for them. Her only attempt, so far, to indicate her feelings on the matter had been the somewhat snide remark, 'You sure give your kids a lot'. She felt guilty that she was so uncharitable about John's generosity toward his children, but she couldn't stop her resentment. This became a problem because she wasn't dealing with it, and it began to interfere with the relationship.

She went to a friend for advice. Her friend said, 'Just imagine for a moment that you are a third person looking down at yourself. There you are—Katherine and John having a romantic dinner. John's telling Katherine about the latest special toy he has bought for one of his sons. Katherine's getting hot under the collar, wishing John would stop all that. She is debating whether she should ask him not to buy so many gifts. Or should she simply give up on the whole relationship and leave it? What would you recommend she do: Leave the relationship? Just sit and say nothing? Tell him to stop buying expensive

gifts? Tell him not to tell her about the gifts?'

Katherine found the bird's-eye view of the problem helpful. She looked at her friend and said, 'Why doesn't she find out why he does it?'

The next time John mentioned a gift he'd bought, Katherine held back the acid remark about to slide off her tongue and instead said: 'I've noticed you buy a lot of expensive gifts for your children. I've often wondered why you do that. Why do you?' She carefully kept her tone of voice neutral.

He thought about it for a while and then replied, 'It helps me feel OK about myself as a father. My own father was incredibly stingy with me, with his time and his money. I vowed I'd be different with my own children. You know what my test is for a good toy? I always choose toys I can relate to the children over. They're things we assemble together, or we all have to go off to a park to use. I think, in part, I'm making up for all those lost opportunities with my own dad.' They talked further about all this. Katherine talked about her childhood and the attitude to toys she grew up with. They weren't trying to change each other's opinions, but simply to hear them.

Finally, John said: 'It's good to feel free to talk about myself so openly.' She was glad she'd responded to her discomfort and found out more. It would have been so easy to have shut down instead. Katherine now felt closer to him than ever.

These are the listening skills you will particularly need to focus upon to draw out information:

- **Ask questions**—Find out specifically what they mean about needs, instructions, context, timing, costs, and so on. Often it's a matter of knowing the right questions to ask.
- **Check back**—to be sure you have heard and understood the relevant details.
- **Summarise**—to make sure you both agree on the facts. In conflict and negotiation one of the most common errors is to jump to conclusions or make assumptions without having enough background information.

If you are the *speaker* and want to check if you are understood, don't ask 'Did you understand?' You may well get a 'yes' answer and you still won't know how much they understood. Ask something like: 'I want to check if you got my message clearly. Can you repeat it back to me?'; 'I'm not sure if I communicated to you all the information. Please tell me what you've understood so far'; or 'Is there anything more you'd like to know?'

If you are the *listener*, remember there are different images and meanings associated with many words. Make sure you get the right message by asking questions. Constantly check exactly what the other person meant. Ask questions that will give you specific information, such as 'How much does it cost?'

Affirmation

Let the other person hear what they are saying.

Have you ever needed a friendly ear, someone to offload your troubles to, someone to just listen? You didn't need advice so much as affirmation—their recognition of your situation. In other words, you needed a sounding-board.

Here, the speaker's aim is to talk about the problem. The listener's aim is to acknowledge the speaker's feelings and thereby help them hear what they are saying. This is of great benefit to the speaker. When you use active listening skills for the purpose of affirmation, focus on the following:

- **Explore** the problem to unfold the difficulty in more depth if time permits. Often we don't know what we think until we express it to someone else. When we feel understood we can move forward.
- **Check** with them about their feelings as well as the facts, e.g. Them: 'She didn't ring to say she wasn't coming.' You: 'How do you feel about that?'; 'How did that affect you?'
- **Paraphrase** the other person's feelings, and perhaps the content of their problem, with a single statement of acknowledgment. Paraphrases are probes to extract a 'yes, that's how it is' response. It helps them to confirm or correct their perceptions when they hear it from you.
- **Try again**. If you misunderstand, ask an open question such as, 'How *do* you see the situation?'; or, 'I don't seem to have it quite right. Tell me again.'
- **Redirect** the conversation if the other person drifts away from the point. They might wander from the topic if they feel you don't understand, or if they don't realise yet what matters most to them.
- **Be careful using the phrase 'I understand you.'** We don't always understand another person's situation. It's usually safer to say: 'I can see that . . .', 'I can relate to . . .', 'It sounds as

if it's been hard for you', 'I don't really know what you must
be going through, but I can see that you're really upset.'

- **Maintain their privacy.**. Using active listening will sometimes
entice people to say more than they intend. Afterwards, they
may become extremely embarrassed and shut down the
relationship. You may need to make sure they really want to
tell you about the problem. You may need to reassure them
about privacy—be sure to keep your word about that.
- **Try to keep the conversation to the point.** Another risk
with active listening is that once some people open up they
won't stop. The more you reiterate what they are saying, the
more they ramble on. You need some sanity-saving sentences
up your sleeve such as: 'Is the point you are making . . . ?';
'I'm getting lost, what is the point that you are making?'; 'I think
what you are saying is very important. I'm sorry, I've run out
of time to hear you out fully. Have you reached any conclusions?'
- **Allow silences** to occur naturally in the conversation.
- **Notice body movements** and sighs as these often indicate
insight or acceptance, and let the person adjust their thinking.
Then ask something like 'How does it all seem to you now?'

Remember that active listening helps the other person focus
beyond their previous way of describing the unresolved issues.
They are sorting things out as they talk to you.

Inflammation

What do you do when the other person is screaming at you? If
you've tried screaming back you probably will have found that often
it makes it all worse. They're inflamed enough already without you
adding fuel to the fire.

When someone complains to you, criticises you, or attacks you,
they are out to tell you that *you* are the problem. You, the listener,
must let them know that you have heard them accurately and have
taken in what they are saying. The purpose is to defuse the hostility
and deal with the problem. The most useful response you can make
is active listening.

*Do they know that
you've heard them
accurately?*

- **Don't defend yourself or retaliate**—at this point it will
inflame them further.
- **Deal first with their emotions**. People sometimes shout
because they don't think they are being heard. Let them know
you understand what their complaint is and how angry or upset
they are. Some useful phrases are: 'It's making you really mad';
'I can see how upset you are'; 'You feel as though you've reached
your limit'; 'Have I got it right? So when I . . . you get really
frustrated with me.'

SARAH'S STORY

My husband Paul and I have a really good relationship. It was really tested, though, when his business went through a very rough patch. It looked as if it could fail altogether. I knew he was worried. We talked about it every day. It was great to be able to support him like that—I felt we were a real team. One evening he told me that Barbara, an old girlfriend of his, had rung him that day. She was offering to work with him and help build up the business again. He asked me what I thought he should do. I knew Barbara. She was very competent and experienced, but I wasn't at all sure of her motives toward Paul. Was she still after him?

I was feeling very threatened. I'd loved to have said, 'Tell her to go away!' I didn't want Paul employing an old girlfriend. But the whole thing was a very touchy situation. If I demanded that Paul didn't employ Barbara, how would he react? He might do the opposite, or blame my jealousy for his

business going further downhill. The one thing I could see was that I dared not give any sort of advice.

I asked Paul some gentle questions to help him consider all the aspects. He soon realised he needed to know what Barbara's real expectations were before he could make a decision. He organised a meeting with her. Paul said she came along to it 'seduction incorporated'—the perfect make-up, the tight dress, the sexy glances. Paul saw that work was only an excuse for what was really on her mind. That was exactly as I suspected, but it seemed a good time to say nothing and keep listening.

Was I relieved when Paul told me he'd rejected Barbara's offer! I was pleased with how I'd handled the situation. I'd left him making all his own decisions. I'd been just the sounding-board. Active listening is certainly a great support to our marriage!

ROGER'S STORY

I had helped my co-worker, Brian, to prepare a proposal which he was to submit to our boss. A week or so later, I still hadn't heard from him how the proposal went. I thought I'd see if Brian wanted any more help. I called in to his office. He was so short with me, it was downright rude. He seemed to resent my enquiry and said he had lots of things on his plate. He accused me of being pushy. I was hurt as I had only meant to be efficient and interested. I know I didn't mean to be pushy at all! I started defending myself. I told him: 'I'm not pushy, I'm just wanting to know how it's going.' He interrupted me. Now he was really stirred up. 'See, you are pushy. I don't know if I want to work with you on it any more.' I got out of his office fast. I was really angry. The moment I had started defending myself he had gone off the deep end. He had mentioned how overloaded

he was. I guess I hadn't really listened to that, once I started reacting to his 'pushy' accusation.

After allowing myself a recovery period, I tried again. 'How are you, Brian?' He replied, 'I'm feeling terribly overworked.' This time I tried active listening, saying, 'I'm really sorry to hear that.' In response he volunteered further information: 'Oh, that meeting to consider our proposal has been postponed. There are other priorities ahead of it at the moment.' I could accept that comfortably. On reflection, I realised that had I attended to what was happening to him in the first place, I would have saved myself a lot of pain and the situation wouldn't have escalated. The real issue was not that I was being too pushy, but that Brian was feeling too much pressure.

- **Acknowledge their point of view**—This does not mean you agree with them, only that you hear, e.g. 'I can see that if you think that was my attitude why you are so angry'; 'I can see why the problem makes you so upset'.
- **Draw them out further**. Explore gently with them to see if there is more behind the emotion. Reaffirm their point as accurately as you can until they calm down. If you do it well, they will explain everything in detail more calmly.
- **Explain, your side of things** without denying they have a problem too, but wait until the heat is out of the conversation.
- **Ask what could be done now** to improve things. If they heat up again, go back to active listening.

How often have you really wanted to connect with someone and it just wouldn't happen? There are deep issues in the way. We'll explore these further in Chapter 6 (Managing Emotions) and Chapter 7 (Willingness to Resolve). When there is real communication, real empathy, a very important interchange takes place below consciousness.

CHRISTINE'S STORY

The relationship with my youngest son was awful. I'd divorced and was living with a new man, Robert. Robert also has children from his previous marriage, but neither of us have our children living with us full-time. Both sets of children come and stay very regularly, however. Unfortunately, my son David, who's 11, was getting on very badly with Robert's son, Paul, who's 9. I think David was jealous of Paul somehow.

Another fight had erupted between the boys. First it was just words, but then they started throwing things at each other. It was getting dangerous. I moved in on the scene. I felt protective toward Paul, who was younger and getting the worst of it. It was easier somehow to lay down the law with my own son. 'David,' I said, 'how dare you throw things at Paul'. David turned and ran out the front door. I panicked, thinking, 'What can I do now? If I don't handle it I will lose it all—the relationship with Robert as well as with David.' I took off after David. It was pouring outside. I called out, 'Don't do this!' I couldn't tolerate it, there was too much at stake. I stopped suddenly and became very determined. I calmly said in a very loud voice, 'If you run away and don't look at what's going on—we might not get another chance to talk.'

It worked. David stopped. He came back toward me, took one look at me standing in the rain and started yelling at me about how I loved Paul more than him, how I took his side all the time, and so on. He had his arms folded across his chest. He wasn't letting me near him. He accused me of telling lies. I took the bait and started defending myself. There we were screaming at each other in the street with rain and tears running down our faces.

I realised that this wasn't working. I had to do something different, fast. Nothing I could have said then would have convinced him that he wasn't right. It flashed into my head that he needed to know he was being heard.

Maybe this was more important than justifying my position right now. So I asked him, 'Isn't it working out for you? Aren't you happy?'

He hedged. 'Yes! No! Umm . . . Sort of . . . Well, not quite.' There was obviously more he wanted to say and it wasn't really clear in his own head. Then he came out with: 'Sort of . . . but I'm missing you.'

Gently, I invited him to come back inside to my room so we could have some time together alone—just the two of us.

He knew I'd heard and he calmed down. Once we were alone together and dried off, we talked about other options in the living arrangements. We explored whether he should come and live with me right now. He'd have to change schools and leave his brother and sister and friends, and he began to see that he didn't want to do that yet.

We were getting back to how we used to be with each other—able to talk things out together. That was precious and lately it had got lost.

I wanted him to see the positive side. I said to him, 'Just think how lucky we are, because although you don't see me every day, when you do—I'm not all caught up in the cooking, and now when we are together we can concentrate on being mates together.'

Finally, he started to soften. He smiled tentatively. To me, it was the most joyous thing I'd seen in ages. I really loved him very much. I'd missed him a lot too, and told him so. I also told him about my plans for us. I was working to save money to build a room for him. I saw him responding with growing interest. I realised I'd never actually said these things to him before.

We ranged across a whole lot of topics. It was a really rich time. When we finished talking, David's parting words were: 'I was planning to go out with a friend tomorrow. Maybe we'll take Paul too.' We'd seen our way through to a new level of adjustment.

SUMMARY

What Cools Communication? Communication killers, like criticism, name-calling and untimely advice, are bad conversation habits that can block empathy.

You won't get away with them if they make the other person feel that you don't respect them. Your real communication is the response you get.

What Warms Communication? Work on the relationship separately from the problem. Empathy openers are conversation topics or activities that give you something safe to share.

Hear how things are for the other person. Use active listening for information (check the facts); affirmation (so the other person can hear what they are saying); and inflammation (so they know you've heard them accurately).

NOTES

1. See more on manipulation in Chapter 5, Co-operative Power.
2. For more on active listening see Gerard Egan, *The Skilled Helper* (California: Brooks/Cole, 1975) and Eugene Gendlin, *Focusing* (U.S., Everest House, 1978).

CHAPTER FOUR

Appropriate Assertiveness

Good conflict resolution requires you to be able to state your case without arousing the defences of the other person. Explain how things are for you rather than what others should or shouldn't do.

It's 5 o'clock. Your train goes in 10 minutes. Your boss wants you to photostat his 50-page draft. You'll miss your train. What will you do?

The phone rings. It's a friend who always talks too long. You're busy. What will you say?

The children pull faces and rebel when you ask for help with the washing up. How will you handle it?

Your neighbour appears to have thrown builders' rubble into some uncleared land at the back of your house. How will you respond?

Every day we're faced with situations that require us to be assertive. Our time is encroached upon. We're not getting what we need. We don't get the help we deserve. Our rights are abused. Do you find yourself attacking before you can stop yourself? Do you respond differently to different people? Which key people in your life are most likely to trigger an attack reaction? How often are you likely to do the following?

——— TICK ———

Behaviour	Rarely	Sometimes	Frequently	People most likely to get this reaction from me
Explode violently	. . . .	. . . .	. . . .	. . . .
Shout	. . . .	. . . .	. . . .	. . . .
Talk over the other person	. . . .	. . . .	. . . .	. . . .

Behaviour	TICK			
	Rarely	**Sometimes**	**Frequently**	**People most likely to get this reaction from me**
Interrupt	. . . .	. . . .	. . . .	. . . .
Insist I'm right	. . . .	. . . .	. . . .	. . . .
Prove my point	. . . .	. . . .	. . . .	. . . .
Nag	. . . .	. . . .	. . . .	. . . .
Put the other person straight	. . . .	. . . .	. . . .	. . . .
Issue ultimatums ('You do it or else')	. . . .	. . . .	. . . .	. . . .
Get even	. . . .	. . . .	. . . .	. . . .
Make acid comments	. . . .	. . . .	. . . .	. . . .
Hurl insults	. . . .	. . . .	. . . .	. . . .

These are fight mechanisms.

Do you more often avoid the problem or postpone doing something about it? How often and with whom do you do any of these?

Behaviour	——TICK——			
	Rarely	Sometimes	Frequently	People most likely to get this reaction from me
Tell someone off at home when you should be sorting it out with someone at work	. . . .	. . . .	. . . .	. . . .
Tell someone off at work when you should be sorting it out with someone at home	. . . .	. . . .	. . . .	. . . .
Dwell on how unfair they are	. . . .	. . . .	. . . .	. . . .
Complain behind their backs but say nothing to their face	. . . .	. . . .	. . . .	. . . .
Withdraw physically	. . . .	. . . .	. . . .	. . . .
Go silent	. . . .	. . . .	. . . .	. . . .
Get depressed	. . . .	. . . .	. . . .	. . . .
Get sick	. . . .	. . . .	. . . .	. . . .
Act superpolite	. . . .	. . . .	. . . .	. . . .
Tell yourself you're not being fair on the other person if you say something	. . . .	. . . .	. . . .	. . . .
Busy yourself with something else hoping the problem will go away	. . . .	. . . .	. . . .	. . . .
Tell yourself it doesn't matter anyway	. . . .	. . . .	. . . .	. . . .

These are flight mechanisms.

Take this example: Someone who lives with you shouts at you. You may understand why they are angry but you hate being shouted at. You've got three choices. You can shout back, withdraw or become appropriately assertive. Shouting back is 'fight'. It's aggressive. It often damages the relationship further. Withdrawal is 'flight'. It's passive. It frequently leaves you alienated from the other person.

If *fight* is your more frequent reaction, are these some of the considerations that go on in your mind?

- Why do I need to be in control?
- What would I feel if I found out I was wrong?
- Do I make myself feel good by proving I am better than others?
- Do I feel that everyone should have the same values as me?
- Should I perhaps question some of my own opinions? What's not working for me any more?

If *flight* is your standard reaction to conflict, in what way are some of these questions relevant for you?

- When I don't say something when I'm irritated, do I really think that they don't sense that I'm upset?
- What damage to the relationship is my withdrawal causing?
- Is it fear or habit that prevents me from speaking?
- Are my feelings as important as the other person's?
- Am I so angry that nothing I say may be very appropriate?
- How frightened am I of their anger?
- How frightened am I of damaging the relationship?
- What's the worst that can happen if I speak?

There is a third option, and that is to *flow*. It's not backing down, but it's non-combative. This flow response isn't always easy. It often requires a conscious choice, a degree of flexibility and skill, some courage and trust in the process of communication. As you become more aware of your communication patterns you will notice sooner when you have taken on a *fight* or *flight* mode. You can use these reactions as your cue to try, as soon as possible, a more appropriate and assertive response.

What do you do?
Fight?
Flight?
or Flow?

It's often hard to break old patterns and try something different. What do you say and how do you say it so that you won't make a situation worse? You need an appropriately assertive statement that will improve things rather than inflame them. For example, 'I'm feeling a bit uncomfortable. Is there anything we need to clear up between us?'; 'Is there anything we need to discuss before the meeting so that it will all flow smoothly?'; or 'I'm feeling concerned about how little we've said to each other over the last few days. I like it better when we tell each other more about what's going on.'

The statements sound simple, but they take a bit of thought. Could a similar diplomatic comment make a difference to the relationship with someone in your life?

Becoming Unconsciously Skilled

Acquiring any skill is usually a four-stage process. Take learning to ride a bike. First, there is a time before you even wanted to learn to ride a bike. You are *unconsciously unskilled*. One day, bike riding suddenly seems interesting but you realise you don't know how to do it. There's a new skill for you to learn. You have moved to *consciously unskilled.*

You take bike riding lessons—start off in a fairly safe place—you're on the way. Within an hour or so you can now sort of drive this two-wheeled contraption from one end of the park to the other without falling off—sometimes. It requires a great deal of attention, but you can do it. You are *consciously skilled.* It may be months before you move to top gear in the learning process, when you no longer have to pay attention to the mechanics of bike riding. Now you steer around obstacles easily and automatically. Stones and potholes are taken in your stride. It has become part of your way of being. Now you are *unconsciously skilled* about bike riding.

The same learning process applies to communication skills when we want to change the way we respond to certain situations.

'I' STATEMENTS

There is a special way of saying how you, personally, respond to a situation which can be very helpful in communicating assertively. It is a formula called an 'I' statement and often needs a lot of practice until it becomes your normal, unconsciously skilled way of saying things.

Don't give up too soon if the method doesn't seem natural—nor was riding a bike, remember. Even the so-called natural responses we make now were once learned, usually by copying the style of parents, teachers, brothers and sisters.

Explain what the situation is for you.

An 'I' statement tells the other person how you feel about something without blaming and without demanding that the other person change. 'I' statements are about *flow*, your third option. They help you to hold your ground without treating the other person as an opponent. If someone is standing on your toe, you might just yell 'Move!' It works for toes but not nearly so well on someone who has left their mess on your desk if you're trying to keep a friendly relationship going. It might be more appropriate to try: 'When your papers are lying on my desk, I feel irritated. I would like to find my desk as I left it.'

Any time is a good time to use an 'I' statement, but it can be particularly effective when you are angry, irritated, upset or just not getting what you want.

An 'I' statement has a structure that is most useful when you want to express yourself about a situation or say what you want. It can be particularly useful when you want to say something to someone, but you don't want them to become defensive. Constructing an 'I' statement is like mixing together cooking ingredients. Using a recipe is more likely to ensure you get it right to start with.

For the 'I' statement recipe there are three ingredients:

1. The action.
2. Your response.
3. Your preferred outcome.

When . . .
I feel . . .
And what I'd like is
that I . . .

The Action

The recipe calls for an objective description of the action or situation that's causing you the problem. Objective, here, means that the description is free of subjective or emotive words. It is a factual description of what happened, not your or anyone else's interpretation of it. Begin with:

'When there are papers left on my desk . . .'
'When I hear a raised voice . . .'
'When I'm not told we are having someone to dinner . . .'

Less objective ways of saying the same thing are:

'When you leave your junk all over my desk . . .'
'When you rant and rave at me . . .'
'When you don't even bother to tell me you've asked one of your friends to dinner . . .'

The last three ways of saying things are a bad start—the other person might be too busy defending themselves to hear the rest of what you are saying. When we are angry with someone, it's quite a challenge to describe their behaviour objectively. Sometimes it helps if the action part of your statement focus on what the problem is for you.

'When I have to sort my papers out from someone else's . . .'
'When I hear someone shouting at me . . .'
'When I don't know about dinner guests . . .'

It's harder for the other person to refute the statement when it is put as a problem. The point is, you still have to clear up your desk, no matter who put papers over it, or why.

An objective description of the event can actually serve the other person. They may not have been aware of what they were doing, or how it affected you. They may have simply meant to emphasise something but you interpreted it as shouting.

Describing specific behaviour objectively can be difficult. Expressions like 'When you accuse me . . .' or 'When you use underhand tactics . . .' reveal your *interpretations* of the experience. The task is to describe the specific behaviour that seems accusatory or underhanded. What is the evidence, the clue? By 'accuse', do you mean someone said you did something that you didn't do? By 'underhand tactics' do you mean someone did something without asking you first?

Your Response

People don't always know how you respond unless you tell them. It's no good saying 'they ought to know'. They *don't* necessarily know what has offended you.

Most people prefer to keep onside with someone else and not to offend, hurt or annoy, so your negative response usually prompts them to reconsider their behaviour, as long as you have not attacked them in the process. When you are talking about your response you know you're on safe ground. You're discussing the facts. People are less likely to argue the point if you say 'I feel tired' or 'I feel frustrated'.

1. Your response might be *an emotion.* For example, you might explain that you feel hurt/angry/ignored/helpless or guilty.

It's sometimes quite hard to find just the right words for how you feel, especially if you are having trouble identifying the feeling. Many people can't label their feelings easily.

2. Telling people what you *do* can sometimes be easier than saying how you *feel.* For example, 'I withdraw'; 'I scream at you'; 'I do everything myself'.

People don't always feel good about telling a boss about their feelings. In some situations it is culturally inappropriate. When you're negotiating it's not always a good idea to let the salesman know how badly you want that car. Describing your actions can sometimes be easier, socially and strategically.

3. Your response might be *an impulse* which, in fact, you resist. You might tell the other person what you feel like doing. For example, 'I feel like ignoring you'; 'I want to walk out'; or 'I wish I could give up.'

Are your 'I' statements clean?

The flavouring in the response ingredient is very important. It's actually quite hard to structure a response without stirring in that element of blame:

'You made me drop it.'

'He made me upset.'

'She hurt my feelings.'

'He drives me mad.'

'It makes me angry.'

It's best to avoid sentences like these.

If you blame others for how you feel, they usually get very defensive and reject the accusation with statements like: 'If you got angry, that's your problem!' 'It's not my fault if every little thing makes you upset.' You can get a lot of unnecessary flak. You need to watch carefully to make sure that your 'I' statements are 'clean', that is, without overt or implied blame.

MADELINE'S STORY

Madeline and her 16-year-old daughter Vivienne lived together, just the two of them (Madeline's husband had left many years ago). They were great friends and proud of their good relationship, which they worked at putting on adult terms. Instead of Madeline making the rules, they made agreements about things like housework, and how to share and respect each other's belongings.

Madeline worked in public relations and some days things were more chaotic and demanding than she could handle comfortably. After one of those days Madeline was greeted at home by Vivienne, who had lots she wanted to tell her. All Madeline heard was Vivienne going on and on with: 'me, me, me . . . I did this . . . then I . . . and I want . . . then I . . .'

Madeline was desperate for some peace and quiet after her hectic day. She looked around the room, noticed the TV was not in its place and said to Vivienne, 'Is the TV still in your bedroom? I thought we had an agreement about it being returned to the lounge.'

Vivienne walked out in a huff. Madeline now had at least the quiet she wanted, but she didn't feel a bit comfortable about the way she had got it.

As it happened, amongst the many things Madeline was squeezing into her busy week was a Conflict Resolution course. The topic that very day had been appropriate assertiveness! She picked up her notes and saw exactly what she had done. She had got what she wanted by attack on her part, and defensiveness and withdrawal from her daughter. What she'd really wanted was her need for quiet to be acceptable.

Madeline took her notes to Vivienne, saying, 'Look what I learned today. What I really wanted to say to you was that when I get home after a day at work, I often feel frazzled and I would like to have some quiet to unwind before I do anything else'.

Vivienne responded with a smile, 'Sure, mum, that seems fair enough.'

When you take responsibility for the way you respond, and avoid blaming others, communication about a problem has a better chance of staying on target. Taking responsibility can make the difference between reacting and responding.

It doesn't mean that you're not entitled to feel what you feel, yet people try to talk themselves out of their feelings: 'I know I shouldn't react like that'; 'I'm silly to feel like that'. When you're making an 'I' statement you give yourself the right to feel exactly how you feel—just don't blame anyone else for it in the process.

Your Preferred Outcome

When you express what you want, try saying: 'I'd like it if I could have adequate help with the washing up'. Discuss what you would like to be able to do or have. We've found this format somewhat safer than: 'I'd like you to help me with the washing up'.

When you tell other people what they should do, they often resist. If they don't feel free to choose, they may resist your suggestion just because autonomy is so important to them. This is often the unmet need behind teenage rebelliousness. Expecting invites resisting.

When we don't like something as it is, we often want someone else to fix it or change it so we feel better. As long as we depend on others like this, we are not in control of our own lives. A thought worth considering: 'For things to change, first I must change.'

They may then change, or they may not, but it will matter less whether they do or don't—the perfect 'I' statement updates them about *you*. When you talk about your preferred outcome—the third ingredient of the 'I' statement—keep as many options open as possible. If you are clear about what you want to be able to do, the other person can see more clearly who can contribute and how.

If I need help with the washing up, there are several ways I can get that. One family member may help per night. We may get a housekeeper, or eat out more often, or buy a dishwashing machine.

A true 'I' statement, in which what you want is not totally dependent on the other person doing something to make you feel better, will also have the effect of opening other options.

A young friend who had recently moved into her first flat told me how her neighbour kept his dogs locked up. They barked a lot throughout the night and kept her awake. She also told me that her neighbour was quite aggressive and that she was scared of him. She asked me whether she should call the RSPCA. I suggested that perhaps she should try an 'I' statement first. We worked on it together. We reached, 'When I hear the dogs barking a lot at night,' (rather than 'when you keep your dogs locked up . . .') 'I feel distressed, and what I'd like is . . .' She thought for a while. 'What *would* you like?' I asked her. Suddenly her face lit up and she said, 'Hey, I'd like to take the dogs for a walk! It would be good for them and for me, and I feel that I could quite comfortably say that to my neighbour.'

Recipe Variation: Reasons

. . . because . . .

You may want to add some explanation to ingredient 3 (your preferred outcome). Frequently the explanations can further aprise the other person of the effect the problem is having on you or of the consequences of the problem. This usually speeds up someone's appreciation of your point of view. Explanations encourage understanding and personal initiative. Many independent and strong-willed children are more willing to co-operate when they thoroughly understand the reasons for a particular rule.[1]

When Do You Use an 'I' Statement?
If you want to say something but don't know how, the 'I' statement formula is a good start. You might want to work it out quite carefully before you see the person. As you work it out you will get so much clearer about what you really need. Your 'I' statement is not about being polite, soft or nice, but nor should it be rude. It's about clarity.

NAN'S STORY

Nan was upset when she heard her son Tommy had visited town and not bothered to call or see her. They seemed to be growing further apart, and she had been brooding over this. She did not want to appear to nag him, nor say anything that would make things worse—but she did want to see him when he came to town.

When next they spoke, instead of putting on her 'pretending not to be hurt' voice she prepared herself for the conversation with an 'I' statement. She had worked on it for quite a while before she got it both 'clear' and 'clean'. She had a clear intention the conversation would be different from all those times when she had only hinted at the problem.

'When I miss out on seeing you I feel hurt and I'd like to see you when you are in town.'

She said it. Tommy immediately reacted with, 'You're always going on at me with the same old thing.'

But this time Nan had a clear intention. 'No,' she said, 'this time I said something different. I was simply telling you how I felt.'

For the first time on this issue, he really heard her. There was a moment's silence. Then instead of getting defensive, his normal pattern, he said 'Well, actually I've tried to phone a few times. You weren't home.' She acknowledged that that was so. She felt much better and they then held the best conversation they had had in ages.

It's not your last word on the subject. It's a conversation opener, not the resolution. It's an opener to honest communication and possibilities, and to improving rather than deteriorating relationships.

You can waste inordinate quantities of brain-power debating how the other person will take your 'I' statement. The cleanest 'I' statements are delivered not to force them to fix things but to let them know how you feel on your side and what you need. Don't expect it to fix straight away what's not working, nor expect the other person to respond immediately.

Even when there is no solution, it still feels better when you can use an 'I' statement to let someone know you feel strongly about the issue. People can underestimate how hurt or angry or put out you are, so it's useful if you can say exactly what's going on without making the situation appear better or worse than it is.

Sometimes the most important person you are making the 'I' statement for is yourself! In the process of making yourself clear you can acquire further understanding of yourself. If you missed a chance to deliver an 'I' statement, make another opportunity. The key to good 'I' statements is to make them so often that they become second nature. You will then be unconsciously skilled.

Appropriate Assertiveness

The next time someone shouts at you and you don't like it, resist the temptation to withdraw (maybe slamming the door on the way out). Resist the temptation to shout back. Deal with your own rising anger.

This is the moment for appropriate assertiveness. Take a deep breath, stay centred, feet firmly planted on the ground, and get your mind into 'I' statement gear. Start mixing the three-ingredient recipe:

1. When you raise your voice at me (*action*);
2. I feel humiliated (*response*);
3. What I'd like is to feel fine when I debate an issue with you (*preferred outcome*).

**Are your 'I'
statements clear?**

The best 'I' statement is free of expectations. It delivers a clean, clear statement of your side of things and how you'd like it to be. Then the ball's in the other person's court. What they do now is up to them.

Some 'I' Statements That Have Worked

1. To someone having trouble meeting deadlines:
'When you need more time to finish a task, I need to know as early as possible so that I can re-evaluate my own timing and resources.'

2. Disrupted work timetables:
'When schedules have to be rearranged I get very disorganised, and I'd like to be notified as soon as it happens.'

3. When you are being told rather than being asked:
'When I am told about changes to our plans, I feel I don't count, and I would like to hear about the changes before they are decided.'

4. To an overly strict teacher:
'When you don't praise me I feel hurt, because I really am trying very hard and what I'd like is some encouragement sometimes.'

5. Dealing with children who are slow to get ready in the mornings:
'When I'm going to work I must leave at 8.30 a.m. and I'd like us all to get organised early—then you can play.'

6. When a family member didn't realise how much it mattered when they came home late:
'When you come home late I feel angry and I don't want to be. It would be a big help if I knew beforehand that you were going to be late.'

7. When one household member is feeling overwhelmed by housework:
'When it seems to me that I do more than my fair share of the housework, I feel put upon and I'd like us to have an arrangement that works for both of us.'

8. Someone has done some work for you that hasn't been completed correctly. It's making you mad because they haven't fulfilled their

MARIA'S STORY

Bob had recently married Maria. They were both in their 40s. It was their second marriage. Maria, whose children were now all living away from home, had devoted much of her time over recent years looking after her ageing, widowed mother. Now, after the honeymoon, Bob and Maria were putting a lot of energy into renovating their home and enjoying their relatively new relationship. Maria was spending less time with her mother.

Then Maria's mother broke her arm and became very demanding, just when Maria was most reluctant to have her own life pressured. This put her in conflict with her Greek upbringing and its strong family values. Though her relationship with her mother had so far been good, this time she felt resentful.

She turned to Bob for advice: 'What can I do? Theo and his family live too far away, Con is in America, Angela has got three young children and lots of problems, and Rosie has just got a job because she needs the money—you know how lazy her husband is. So it's pointless asking any of them.'

Bob thought a while. Should she drop everything for her mother and leave the renovations aside for a while? Pay someone to look after her mother (which they could hardly afford)? Ask her mother to contribute? Put the hard word on the other family members?

He finally said, 'Could you just discuss the situation with each of them without asking anything of them? Simply listen to each of them and acknowledge what problems and stresses they have too. Leave them to think what we could all do to help while mum's arm gets better.'

Maria contacted all her brothers and sisters, even Con in America. She started the conversations with an 'I' statement: 'I'm worried that I won't be able to give Mum all the support she needs.' She went on to explain the situation and listen to their own stresses and pressures. She said to Bob, 'Oh well, at least I tried', having listened to their stories and feeling very 'dumped on'. Within the next few days each of Maria's family offered to do something. Angela offered to mind their mother overnight, Rosie offered to take some prepared meals over there and her 'lazy' husband agreed to transport mum to hospital for her treatments (he was a taxi-driver, after all). Even Con in America sent some money for a housekeeping service.

Maria wasn't sure what had made the change until afterwards, when Angela said to her: 'I felt like doing something this time because you seemed to care about me and didn't judge my lifestyle, unlike everyone else in the family. I felt needed, not cast out.' Nor did the others feel pressured or criticised.

Although she had never actually discussed it with her brothers and sisters, Maria had quietly, with some resentment, taken on the whole responsibility of her mother. Each member of the family had made their own interpretations of Maria's silence, and had some unexplored guilt. The family had grown apart over unspoken issues. By the time the broken arm had mended, so had the split in the family.

Maria's 'I' statement was an opener. She didn't know what would happen, but the response was more positive and more far-reaching than she could ever have envisaged.

side of the bargain: 'When I found mistakes in the work, I felt really let down and I would like to get over my anger and feel better about working with you.'

SUMMARY

What do you do? Fight, flight or flow?

Once you've discovered your usual reaction, choose instead to explain how the situation is from your point of view using an 'I' statement.

Is your 'I' statement clean?

Action: Don't use word irritators.

Response: Don't cast blame.

Preferred outcome: Don't phrase it as a demand.

Is your 'I' statement clear?

Action: Say what is *really* the matter.

Response: Indicate the degree of distress you feel (or as much as you feel is appropriate to disclose).

Preferred outcome: Make sure that this is specific enough to allow new options to be developed.

We need to remember that the problem is really our own—no matter what the other person is doing or how justified our complaint. We need to state clearly our own needs and our preferred outcomes.

NOTES

1. Robert Bolton, *People Skills* (Australia: Simon and Schuster, 1987)
2. Thomas Gordon *Parent Effectiveness Training* (N.Y., Wyden, Inc., 1970)

CHAPTER FIVE

Co-operative Power

In this chapter we will look at *power relationships.* We will examine the kind of power dynamics and inbalances relationships can slip into, and how to change to 'power with' instead of 'power over'. We will look at *personal power*—what makes each of us a powerful person.

Take a moment now to orientate yourself to the topic. Ask yourself these questions, and perhaps write down some thoughts:

- What does power mean to you?
- What role does power play in your life?
- Who has power over you?
- Who do you have power over?
- Around whom do you feel powerful?
- What makes you feel powerful?
- Around whom do you feel powerless?
- How do you diminish your power?

'Ultimate power is the ability to produce the results you desire most and create value for others in the process . . . Power is the ability to change your life, to shape your perceptions, to make things work for you and not against you . . . Real power is shared, not imposed . . . It's the ability to define human needs and to fulfil them—both your needs and the needs of the people you care about . . . It's the ability to direct your own personal kingdom—your own thought processes, your own behaviour—so you produce the precise results you desire.'[1]

In personal relationships your power is your ability to have what you want. It is based on many things, including position, the ability to give or withhold what others want, relevant expertise and information, and personal qualities.

POWER BASES

To find out how the different power bases operate, think of people in your life you often comply with, even when you don't really want to—people who tend to influence you to do things their way. What is the basis of their influence over you?

Valued Relationship Do you care about the relationship being friendly? How would it suffer if you did not comply?

Expertise Do you trust their advice because they know more about the matter? What is their special area of competence, information or expertise?

Position Do you respect their authority? How would you describe your respective places in the hierarchy or pecking order?

Reward Do they reward you—openly or covertly—if you agree? Which rewards, if any, influence you?

Punishment Do they punish or censure you in any way? If so, how?

Persuasiveness Do you respect and trust them as individuals? If so, which of their personal qualities do you particularly admire or respect? Is it, for example, their commonsense, their ability to sell an idea well, their charisma, or their integrity?

The use of expertise or rank, the promise of reward, the threat of punishment, the emotional tie to a valued relationship, persuasiveness—all are levers that help people get what they want. These levers can be used fairly or unfairly. Let's use the word 'influence' for legitimate or acceptable leverage. Some people, however, regard influence as a threat to their individuality, while others are so cautious about influencing others that they end up with very little of what they want in life. Co-operation and achieving consensus depend on one side influencing the other. Influence is a necessary process in communication. Nevertheless, if the result is that we feel tricked, used or stood over, then something has gone awry in the influencing process. Let's use the word 'manipulation' for such occasions. What distinguishes manipulation from influence?

MANIPULATION	INFLUENCE
The outcome is generally desirable for the manipulator.	The outcome may or may not affect the influencer.
The outcome is frequently undesirable for the other person.	The willingness of the other person is taken into account.

MANIPULATION	**INFLUENCE**
Information that doesn't support their case is not disclosed.	They are usually given all the facts.
The other person is not left free to choose for themselves	The other person is free to choose

The difference between influence and manipulation is not black or white. We all do a little manipulating from time to time. Whether or not it was acceptable depends upon how positive the outcome was. Did everyone win something in the process?

POWER TRIANGLE

We all operate a range of different power relationships. We have absorbed some of them from past experiences and tradition, such as parent-child, child-teacher, employee-boss, male-female relationships. Sometimes these work well for us, but not when we feel powerless or powerful at the expense of others. It's all too easy for some of us to slip into power games and assume roles.

Transactional analysis[2] defines three roles people can easily get caught up in: *persecutor, rescuer* and *victim.* Are you inclined to fall into any of these traps?

Many people are familiar with the *persecutor* role from their childhood. Parents frequently use their power to solve problems. ('Do it because I said so.') The persecutor's assumption or attitude is: 'I am OK and you are not OK'.[2] To protect themselves from uncertainty and the fear of their own powerlessness, persecutors demand obedience, relying heavily on rewards, punishments and their position of authority. If you grow up copying this kind of behaviour you may discover you play the persecutor role with your own children, your spouse and people you work with. You may not even realise what you are doing. If you realise that you've bulldozed someone with your point of view, you'll know you've played the persecutor role.

The *rescuer* attitude is faulty also because it's a variation on the persecutor's 'I'm OK, you're not OK'. The rescuer assumes that 'other people need my help'—The rescuer needs to be needed. At their best, rescuers give a lot of support. They'll provide a friendly ear for a person in trouble. They'll do all sorts of helpful things such as giving the person time off, or by doing their work or making their choices for them. But when rescuers do *too* much they end up feeling used. When the rescuer sides with the victim problems arise because the rescuer acts as a buffer between the victim and his or her differences, which alienates the victim even further. Rescuers blunder into this trap by their very desire to help when someone they care about feels badly treated.

Some rescuers become addicted to the role and feed off conflict, running from one party to another with nasty reports about each. They assume that anyone they side with in a conflict will like them best. Is it any wonder that rescuers are often turned against by the people they are trying to befriend?

The self-image of the *victim* may be 'I'm not OK, you're OK'; or 'I can't fix things and I need someone to help me.' Their feelings of inadequacy can overwhelm them. There are a number of pay-offs supporting the victim's position: (a) The victim receives lots of help; (b) they collect lots of sympathy; and (c) they don't have to try to fix the problem. Hopelessness can mask the fact that the person feels it's easier and safer to have the problem than to encounter the risks involved in sorting out the difficulty. Under the threat of violence or the withdrawal of love, victims find the risks are sometimes

much too high to try to change things. The trap and the tragedy lie in their ingrained attitudes of self-defeat.

What causes these attitudes? Victims learn to be so from other victims. By demonstration parents teach their own victimhood to their children; authoritarian parents, teachers, bosses and systems can scare people into victimhood; and sometimes cautious habits allow people to slide into becoming a victim because they don't test the situation—or themselves. So they never realise that if they used the right approach they could create positive changes relatively easily.

It is important to distinguish between *role-playing victims* and *genuine victims*. Real victims who suffer from hardship, injustice and accident naturally deserve care and sympathy and need support until they can manage on their own. The skills of conflict resolution are of the utmost significance in addressing power inbalances in a system that leave individuals or groups severely disadvantaged. Real victims deserve to address the injustices done to them. They need all the skills outlined in this book and may even need to use their rights at law. If you are in a mediators role, your first responsibility is to protect the genuine victim. If there is nothing invested emotionally in the underdog position they will begin to respond to support and to help themselves. Role-playing victims seem to attract accidents, mischances and illnesses. The self-appointed rescuer, whose role becomes their ego prop, is easily lured by a self-appointed victim. They're a perfect match until one of them sees the light.

With three or more people in a family or work group, a triangle relationship often develops. It becomes like an improvised stage play, repeated every night. The script varies somewhat but the play is basically always the same. One character is the 'baddie'. The least powerful person—perhaps a child or an adult with low self-esteem— plays the 'innocent victim' and the third person takes on the role of rescuer, defending the victim from the persecutor. When they get bored they might swap roles around for a while or rope in other people to play them. In some families the drama includes physical violence. In others it's more sedate and involves subtle put-downs, innuendos and private 'hate sessions'.

Does an early power triangle play re-runs in your life? Do you ever feel you are dealing with a pack of fools who, without your firm hand, would stray? Is there someone you frequently rant about, in their absence, along the 'Ain't it awful' theme? Are you feeling badly done by but you haven't done anything to fix it? Watch yourself for signs of the persecutor, rescuer or victim roles, and examine the attitudes underlying them.

There are alternate ways to act out the relationships involved in

Taking responsibility: Persecutor teaches Rescuer mediates Victim learns.

POWER GAME TRIANGLE

PERSECUTOR
'I'm OK. You're not OK.'
'It's got to be your fault.'
- Often get what they want in the short term.
- Long-term relationships usually out of balance.

RESCUER
'I'm OK. You're not OK.'
'Other people are inadequate. They need my help.'
- Often offers unwelcome help.
- Often ends up rejected or used.

VICTIM
'I'm not OK. You're OK.'
'I can't fix things and I need someone to help me.'
- Very dependent
- Not happy and with a low self-esteem.

DISCOVERY TRIANGLE

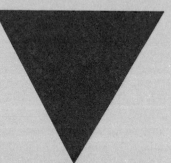

TEACHING
Show the other person what will work best for everyone—and explain why.
- Invite and respect the other person's point of view.
- Give up threats, attaching blame and sulking.

MEDIATING
Encourage people to settle their differences.
- Support people who are defending and helping themselves.
- Look at the wider context and see how much help is (and is not) appropriate.

LEARNING
Use even the most difficult situation as a learning opportunity.
- Start with one thing that will make a positive difference.
- Celebrate your growing ability to stand up for yourself.

the power triangle. Once you take responsibility for your power relationships you can transform these roles by rejecting their negative, harmful aspects. By changing attitudes the *persecutor* can *teach*, the *rescuer* can *mediate*, the *victim* can *learn*.

Acting in these ways you can choose how you can relate to people in the other two corners. If I am a victim and choose to learn, then I can choose to see my persecutor as a teacher.

The power triangle can launch you into discovery and the creative response described in Chapter 2. New possibilities and solutions then replace superiority, the compulsion to feel needed, and helplessness.

STANLEY'S STORY

I am a headmaster in a small country town. A new teacher had just been appointed to my school. I encouraged him to come to me with any difficulties. The teacher soon came to me with a big predicament—he had punished a consistent troublemaker in his class, but now he realised that the punishment had been too severe. The child had complained to his parents, who were irate, and soon the word would be all around town. A classic victim-persecutor-rescuer game threatened.

Instead of deciding who was right or wrong, I became a mediator. I called together all the parties involved. I supported the teacher's acknowledgment to the child and parents that he regretted what he had done (thus allowing him to avoid being seen either as a persecutor of the child or victim of the headmaster or town's sanction). And I encouraged the child to see that he had provoked his teacher and that though people make mistakes, amends can be made and new relationships formed. This took the child and parents into the learner position and a constructive discussion followed on how teacher, child and parents could find better ways of relating to each other.

FROM POWERLESSNESS TO POWER

As a victim you may get lots of sympathy and avoid responsibility, but any step towards self-help takes you from powerlessness towards power. It transforms the victim into a learner, discoverer, explorer. 'What is one thing I can do to improve this situation?' is the question to answer.

Emerging from the victim role means facing a challenge. Few persecutors throw off their obsession with control willingly. They are used to being the winners in direct confrontation, and don't take kindly to a frontal attack. Transforming a persecutor takes more skill but can be more effective in the long term than defeating them. Persecutors make dangerous enemies. Can you redress the injustice and keep the persecutor on side?

Confronting Powerful People

Of course, not all powerful people are role-playing persecutors. Whether or not the person uses power as an emotional crutch, the strength of their powerbase makes them hard to confront.

What can you do when a more powerful person says 'no' to you?[3] Here are some strategies:

1. Think of ways to help them trust you. For example, talk to them more frequently; tell them what's important to you.

Redirect the agenda to the win/win approach.

2. When you talk to them about the issue be very clear about your purpose and direction and remember:
   (a) You want everyone's needs considered.
   (b) Use objective yardsticks to judge what is fair rather than engaging in a clash of wills.
   (c) Aim towards a joint problem-solving approach rather than either side issuing ultimatums.

3. Without threatening, outline clearly the consequences of non-agreement. Be sure of your legal rights and procedures. Find out the likely consequences of their position. What sort of appropriate incentives might persuade them?

4. Work out your alternatives and how to make the best of it if they don't see it your way. It's important not to seem too desperate (see Chapter 10, Negotiation, Best Alternative to a Negotiated Agreement).

5. Coalitions and alliances can be persuasive, so find some supporters.

6. Redirect the energy—opposition can be reframed, as follows:
   (a) Reframe an attack on you as an attack on the problem. For example, 'You stupid idiot!' can be answered with 'What aspect of the problem haven't I taken into account?'
   (b) Avoid directly opposing the other person. Instead of saying 'You're dead wrong', ask 'Have we considered everyone's needs here?'
   (c) Present their opposition or solution as one of several options. For example, reframe 'You'll do it my way' by replying: 'That is certainly one alternative—are there any others that would work for you?'
   (d) Find out what makes them choose that option. For example: 'You say you'd like to use plan X. Tell me why it works for you.'
   (e) Bring to attention other people's needs and values: 'I think we should include Brian's need for more room.'

7. People who misuse power are out to prove they are powerful.

If you don't want to be their target don't verbally attack power-hungry people—feed them with positive reinforcement.

8. Use *active listening* (see Chapter 3, Empathy) to discover their specific needs.

9. Decide which issues are worth fighting about and which are not in the situation. Sometimes the cost of fighting a powerful person is just too high. Sometimes the misuse of power makes you so angry you might find it worth staking everything to oppose it.

PERSONAL POWER

You can distinguish between positional power (which is a consequence of people's positions or roles) and personal power (which is a result of people's personalities). The two do not necessarily go together: some people have positional power yet do not seem to have a lot of personal power—and vica versa.

What does personal power consist of?

Think of someone you know or know of whom you admire for their personal power. Consider some positive qualities on which you feel their personal power is based on.

We've asked this question many times in workshops and have noticed a very interesting thing about the replies people give—they usually name qualities that they would particularly like to develop in themselves. Is is true for you? Can you add to the following?

Successfulness
Energy
A clear sense of direction
Good leadership
Good communication
Charisma
Persuasiveness
Enthusiasm
Calm
Balance
Kindness to others
Logical thinking
A co-operative spirit
An ability to manage rather than suppress emotions
Perception
Wisdom

Many of these qualities have to do with self-mastery.

Disempowering Language

Sometimes the way we use language diminishes our own power.

Instead of	Try
I'm just a housewife.	I am a housewife.
I'm not very good at . . .	I have more to learn about . . .
I'm only new here.	I recently started here.
I just wanted to say . . .	I have something I'd like to add . . .
I don't want to take up your time but . . .	Do you have a little time for me? I have something to discuss.
It's hard when you have three kids and only a small income.	I'm finding it hard with three kids and only a small income.

How often have you said: 'I don't feel like going to work but I have to'; 'I don't want to ring them but I suppose I'd better'; or 'I'm so bored when I visit those people but I know I should go'? What are some of the things you do because you think you should? As well, using the word 'you' (the second person) when you are really referring to yourself has the effect of disowning the experience and the possibilities for changing it.

Masters not Victims

How do you face a task you resist? If you accept the challenge its difficulties present and give it your best, your personal power will grow.

Are you 'shoulding' or choosing?

Each time you face a task turn it into a choice. 'I should watch my son's football game but I want to do the shopping and mow the lawn' can become: 'I choose to give this support to my son. The other tasks can wait.' There's a huge difference in the quality of your companionship when you deliberately make the effort to be there. Children can spot the difference between choice and duty a mile off.

If you attend a meeting because you should attend, the meeting is running you. You can be run by people or situations or even your own ethics ('I should be supportive', 'I should be honest', 'I should be more caring'). This means you're not in charge—external pressure or authority, or the memory of authorities in your past are dominating your decision-making. Have you ever put down the phone thoroughly irritated by a friend telling you what you ought to be doing? One child's comment: 'When my mum says 'must' I feel 'won't' all over'.

You have two options: you can submit or rebel. If you submit

ROBIN'S STORY

I am the mother of two teenage daughters, and I've always resented the amount of time I have to spend in the supermarket doing the family shopping. It always irritated me. I used to stand in those long twisted queues thinking of things I'd rather be doing. One day, standing in a queue and feeling resentful, I found myself looking into someone else's trolley and was appalled at the amount of 'junk' food piled in it. I started thinking about what I was really doing in the supermarket. I wasn't 'just having to do the shopping'—I was choosing to make a

contribution to my family's health. It has always been important to me that they all ate healthy, balanced food and I'd rather choose the food myself than let someone else do it. As I realised that I wanted to do the shopping, I was amazed at what other positive aspects I could find—how fortunate I was that I could buy what I wanted. I even started to make a game of my venture to the supermarket. I began smiling at other shoppers and counted how many smiles I got back!

there's resentment. If you rebel there's resistance, perhaps resentment as well. Both stances sap your energy and encourage some form of revenge. We have to balance our energy budget somehow. If we tend to submit and then seek revenge, we are slipping into the victim role. If we get our way, we become a persecutor (no matter how subtly).

If, on the other hand, we choose to put ourselves through an experience, we are self-directed, and not imposed on. We are autonomous. When life presents a challenge we decide to accept it or not. We feel free, whatever our decision. Here are some more examples of self-directed choice:

Instead of	Try
Mum will be furious if I don't go.	I feel like pleasing my mother by going.
Why should I bother to visit my grandmother in the nursing home? She hardly ever recognises me anyway.	Perhaps just for a few minutes she will realise I cared enough to come—that makes it worth the effort.
It's such a long drive.	I'll take along some good tapes to make the drive pleasant.
I should do the family's ironing.	I'll do the ironing so that everyone looks good. It's one of the ways I show I love them.

Shifting from 'I should' to 'I choose' means you cope better with your own 'shoulds' as well as the 'shoulds' imposed on you by others. You consciously focus on your best reason for doing something

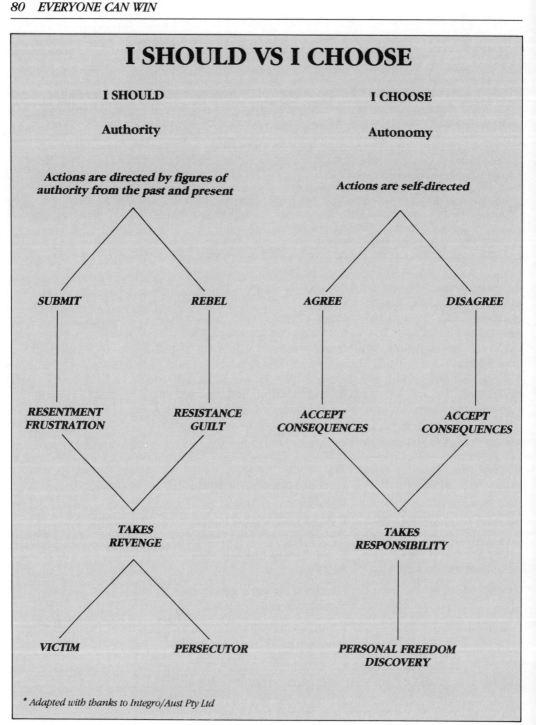

I SHOULD VS I CHOOSE

I SHOULD

Authority

Actions are directed by figures of authority from the past and present

SUBMIT   REBEL

RESENTMENT FRUSTRATION   RESISTANCE GUILT

TAKES REVENGE

VICTIM   PERSECUTOR

I CHOOSE

Autonomy

Actions are self-directed

AGREE   DISAGREE

ACCEPT CONSEQUENCES   ACCEPT CONSEQUENCES

TAKES RESPONSIBILITY

PERSONAL FREEDOM DISCOVERY

* *Adapted with thanks to Integro/Aust Pty Ltd*

('It will make a difference to grandma's day') and do everything you can to support yourself in the process. Right now there are probably several things you don't like doing. If you're doing them anyway, why not choose to do them and free yourself up to enjoy them?

Exercising your own choice this way can make the difference between a great day and a bad one. Applied day after day to a thousand different tasks, it can turn an ineffectual, mundane existence into one of personal power. Personal power blossoms when you want what you have in your life. You can resist or flow with whatever circumstances life presents. Develop the habit on small tasks. When the big challenges come you will be glad you have a personal commitment to operating your life out of choice.

Personal power blossoms when you want what you have in your life.

JANE'S STORY

Not long ago I received a memo from my boss instructing the staff to carry out some new procedures. It was badly phrased, and sounded dictatorial to me and many other staff members. I had two choices—to obey or rebel. Either way, I was going to feel terrible about the disharmony. Was there another way?

It wasn't just an internal shift I had to make. It was necessary to take a stand against that memo. I went to my boss with a carefully worded statement: 'I just want you to know that when I read this I felt like doing the opposite of what you asked—and I don't want to be like that. I want to be supportive and co-operative.' My approach wasn't challenging, but factual.

My boss took it far better than I could have expected. He said, 'That's interesting—which parts made you feel like that?' Then we talked about them. I got a different slant on the situation in this face to face friendly discussion. I left feeling I could now freely choose to follow the new procedures. My boss gained some helpful insights about approaching staff to implement his new plan.

When Jane left the discussion, the relationship had gained a new element—respect—which continued to develop. Her commitment to choice and personal autonomy benefited rather than limited her relationship with external authority.

PAST CONFLICTS

Just as we can make active choices rather than submit to or resist circumstances as they arise in our present lives, so can we also reframe our memories of the past to change the flavour of the present. We can choose to resolve old conflicts. The pain and upset locked away inside can add a sour note to our voice when faced with a new conflict that resembles an old one.

We can reframe a past event many years later. The ability to do this comes when we recognise and accept the long-term value of its consequences.

Empower the present by choosing the past.

ALISON'S STORY

I discovered, to my disgust, that my husband had been regularly making love to another woman—a friend of mine—in our marital bed. Feeling deeply betrayed, I divorced him. I continued bringing up my children. Ten years later I came home early from the office one day, opened my bedroom door and discovered my 17-year-old son making love to his girlfriend in my bed. Memories of old pain came flooding back.

I just could not tolerate him making love to anyone in the family home, let alone my bed, and ranted and raved about his behaviour. Later I regretted the way I'd handled the situation. I realised that my messy divorce had coloured my perspectives

on my son's behaviour. This insight made me suddenly think about the whole episode of my divorce. I realised that today I wouldn't want to be with Don (my ex-husband). I've managed the kids really well without him. My life hasn't always been easy, but I think it has been easier than if I had stayed with Don. I can let the whole divorce drama go now. I don't really blame Don any more for how he is.

After I'd thought it all through, I felt really complete again. A couple of days later I managed a more considered talk with my son and we came to some reasonable agreements.

Has there been a circumstance in your life you still resent? Have any benefits arisen from the situation? If you had to repeat it all again, what would you do differently? What would you leave substantially the same? What else would it take to shift your perspective from resentment to choice?

You are working here towards the freedom that can flow in all parts of your life when you respond with choice rather than resistance.

Using Energy to Empower Yourself

'She's so alive'; 'You're in a black mood'; 'I'm all at sixes and sevens'; 'They're a dead weight'; 'I don't like the vibes'—these are colloquial ways we talk about people's energy. Just as a light bulb is a power source that emits light, so it is for human beings. This energy depends partly on physical health and metabolism but it also has to do with our thoughts and feelings. Physical, emotional and mental activities have energy components which we can sometimes become aware of as vibrations or auras. We are always responding to our unconscious perception of another person's energy as much as what they actually say or do.

When someone uses power over another person, the energy intrudes on the other person's 'energy space'. Such energy abuse usually causes hurt, resentment or anger. You've probably invaded someone's energy space yourself whenever you have insisted on having your own way. When *your* energy space is intruded upon do you submit? If you do your aura collapses—you feel 'squashed' or 'diminished'. A person who has experienced too many 'you musts'

or 'you must nots' for too long has a permanently collapsed energy system. They are likely to feel depressed, suppressed and weakened.

Other people, however, rebel when someone tries to use power over them intrusively. Their rebellious anger gives them a lot of energy, but they also gradually develop a protective armour which can make them insensitive to the needs of those around them. This protective armour is visible in a certain rigidity in the muscles around the chest. It is also reflected at an energy level, so that these self-protective people seem 'prickly' or if you try to talk to them it is like 'talking to a brick wall'.

Equal relationships are very precious. Which of your relationships are like that? An appropriate use of power leaves you and the other person whole and free to choose. From this position you develop co-operative power relationships, in which two people can stand together looking for solutions to their mutual problems. Each person keeps their personal power intact and respects the other person's space and integrity. This is the difference between 'power with' and 'power over'.

People with plenty of personal power are those who do not dissipate it in submission or rebellion. They are whole, and centred— that is, they are totally involved in the here and now. To others they appear very alive and ready for action.

Aiki Principles

Martial arts have long used the principle of physically centring the self as part of the preparation for combat. Some believe the geometric centre of all the forces at work in the human body occurs at a spot about two finger-widths below the navel. The Japanese name for this point is *hara*. Remaining aware of this point even while you attend to what's happening keeps you fully alert and firmly grounded. You don't have to wait for physical combat to discover its usefulness. Try concentrating on your hara next time you feel flustered by too many tasks, or when something has thrown you off-centre.

Centre and flow. Take a moment and try it right now. Touch your belly, just below your navel, and gently press. Focus your energy on where your hand is. When you have established the sensation look around you. You should feel very alert.

The martial art of *aikido* uses centring as a starting point. It teaches you more, too, about handling yourself well in conflict. The name *aikido* is a composition of three Japanese words: *ai* meaning harmony;

LESLEY'S STORY

I'm a fairly asssertive woman but I was at my wits' end over a power relationship at work. My boss, a very intellectual and dogmatic man, continually used his facility with words to argue with me. We had opposing views on religion and feminism and, although I don't usually have difficulty debating issues, I felt that he always talked me down and didn't listen to me. He was like that with everyone and I felt helpless about changing it. But I certainly didn't want it to continue.

Thinking about the problem carefully, I realised that I'd let my energy collapse whenever I was around my boss. I decided that I would have to be quite assertive to hold my ground with him and not be diminished by his forcefulness. I visualised myself maintaining my energy when I communicated with him.

One day I said to him, 'I understand your point of view, but I'm not sure that you understand mine.' I then proceeded to explain my values to him in considerable detail. I wasn't belligerent, but I didn't back down either. I used my own personal power to match his and to demand my right to be treated as an equal.

ki meaning universal energy; and *do* meaning the way.[4] Altogether: 'the way of harmonising with universal energy'.

Aikido works on the principle that a universal force or energy flows through everything. Individuals can align themselves with this force and bring the energy of others into alignment with it also. The purpose of an *aikido* manoeuvre is not to hurt, as it is in some martial arts, but to disarm or divert the attack. Its physical practice resembles a dance as the attacker's energy is deflected and rendered harmless. An *aikido* master is very alert and flows with the energy of his adversary. The expert canoeist does something similar by flowing with the force of rapids and avoiding boulders in the river.

Apply these techniques to everyday conflict in the following ways:

1. Flow with the energy, don't resist it. Your strength is your ability to forego resistance.

2. Dance. Redirect the energy of attack toward the positive. Reframe negatives to their positive counterparts. A glass can be described as half-empty or half-full. Help the other person say what they do want rather than what they don't want.

3. Use the other person's energy even if it appears to be angry or attacking. Find out where it is coming from and support their genuine claims along with your own. Acknowledging the other person's needs can change the relationship dramatically. Welcome their energy as a contribution toward solution: 'I'm so glad you brought that up . . .'; 'We must include the point you are making.' Let them discover themselves to be on your side. Let their contribution unite with yours to provide a broader focus on the problem.

'Power with' rather than 'Power over'.

4. The end purpose is caring and respect. You will sometimes find yourself in the position of teacher and required to set firm limits and prevent or correct unacceptable behaviour. *Aikido* is always loving. As Neem Karoli Baba said, 'Do what you do with another person but never put him out of your heart.'[5]

Eleven Empowering Thoughts

1. 'Life is not anything; it is only the opportunity for something'— Friedrick Hebbel, a German poet. It's what you bring to life that is significant—not what life brings to you.
2. Life can be a continual process of growth and development. If you choose to regard it this way, you add meaning and direction to it.
3. Everything and everyone is on your side if you decide to see it that way.
4. Look for a good intention behind apparent unkind behaviour.
5. Overwhelming events can be opportunities for change and for unfolding new levels of strength and love.
6. Failure is a splendid chance to learn.
7. Success starts with commitment. Everything flows from that.
8. Hold your fear in one hand and your courage in the other. Fear alone is not a good enough reason to avoid something.
9. Align your personal power with life. Accept the present before imagining what might be.
10. Be here now. The point of power is in the present.
11. This is not a rehearsal for your life, this is it.

SUMMARY

1. 'Ultimate power is the ability to produce the results you desire most and create value for others in the process.' (Anthony Robbins)
2. Power may develop from the emotional tie to a valued friendship, the use of expertise or rank, the promise of reward, the threat of punishment, or the person's ability to persuade.
3. We can distinguish between manipulation or influence on the basis of how negative or positive the outcome is for the other person.
4. The roles in the power triangle (persecutor, rescuer or victim) can be transformed to teacher, mediator and learner when people take responsibility for their power relationships.
5. Find ways to redirect the agenda of the powerful, resistant person toward the win/win approach.
6. Personal power is diminished by 'shoulds'.

7. Personal power blossoms when you want what you have in your life.
8. Empower the present by choosing the past.
9. Create equal relationships—'power with' instead of 'power over.'
10. Use *aikido* principles and centre the flow.
11. The aim is co-operative power. 'Do what you need to do with another person but never put them out of your heart.'

NOTES

1. Anthony Robbins, *Unlimited Power* (New York: Simon and Schuster, 1986), pp 20-1.
2. For a Transactional Analysis (TA) explanation of the triangle, see Muriel James and Dorothy Jongeward, *Born to Win* (Signet, New American Library), p 93. Other highly recommended books on Transactional Analysis are Thomas A. Harris, MD, *I'm OK, You're OK* (Pan), and Claude M. Steiner, *Scripts People Lives Lives* (Bantam).
3. See also Roger Fisher and William Ury, *Getting to Yes* (London: Arrow), 1981 pp. 112 ff.
4. Thomas F. Crum, *Magic of Conflict* (New York: Simon and Schuster, 1987) has written a splendid book on the principles of the *aikido* approach to life and conflict.
5. Ram Das, *Miracle of Love* (New York: Dutton), 1979, p. 254.
6. Quoted in Viktor E. Frankl, *The Doctor and the Soul: From Psychotherapy to Logotherapy* (New York: Knopf, 1955), p. 113.

CHAPTER SIX

Managing Emotions— Fires for Change

Have you ever felt:

- So overwhelmed you couldn't think clearly what you wanted to say?
- So outraged you thought something like, 'I'll show them. They'll never do that to me again,'?
- So hurt by someone you could never forgive them?
- So scared you were shaking all over?
- So agitated you couldn't sit still?
- Unable to stop yourself launching into a barrage of abuse?
- Unable to stop someone else abusing you?
- Just about ready to kill someone?
- Just about ready to kill yourself?

Managing emotions: Don't indulge Don't deny Use emotions to build richer relationships.

Our emotions can overwhelm us and sweep us away. Catching hold of them and channelling their energy in a positive direction is what the skill of managing emotions is about.

Don't deny your emotions. It's unrealistic to pretend you don't have a problem when someone has just run into the back of your car. It's not usually a good idea to act unconcerned when your teenager comes home at night two hours late. The fastest way to get an apology when someone has hurt your feelings is to tell them you feel hurt (see Chapter 4, Appropriate Assertiveness). On the other hand, don't indulge in unbridled displays of bad feelings if you want to win friends and influence people. A temper tantrum at work can get you sacked. Take too many of your irritations out on your spouse and the result can be a broken marriage. Wallowing in misery and hurt can get you lots of sympathy for a while, but it can also wear out a good relationship. If you never face up to what makes you fearful, you will certainly feel safer but you may not get what you really want.

For most people, successful living depends on involvement, friendship and intimacy. Our emotions provide the gauge of how that contact is progressing—of what's going right or wrong. When channelled appropriately, our emotions are building richer relationships.

BODYMIND

There is a developing branch of psychology known as Bioenergetics. It rests on a belief in the close correspondence of body and mind. The body's respiration and metabolism create energy which is used for physical movement as well as for emotions and thought.

As electricity runs along wires, so the body's energy is directed to different areas by muscular contraction and relaxation. The intricate and ever-changing patterns of energy flow are reflected in feelings,

Emotions are mind, body and energy events.

thought and action. It's a single process with different manifestations, similar to the way electricity in a light globe manifests both as heat and light. Thus in one sense we don't so much have a body, but we are a body—we are bodymind.[1]

It is often through our body that we become aware of our emotions. Common language bears testimony to this in expressions like 'I feel it in my bones'; 'She makes me sick to my stomach'; 'I've got butterflies in the stomach'; 'He is so open-hearted'; 'You're a pain in the neck'. The body is like a giant computer constantly reading our emotional relationship to other people, the environment and ideas. It throws up on the screen of consciousness each significant response as it arises.

Through the body's energy flows, feelings, thoughts and actions all affect each other. As well as responding to what's happening right now, feelings, thoughts and actions are also fed by deep, unconscious processes—thoughts unformed, relationships unexplored, intimacy unresolved. Energy contained in the body and registered by the way we move is a 'frozen' history of our experience.

The ageing process produces some rigidity in the body, but far more rigidity sets in through the repeated suppression of emotions— fear that wasn't permitted to shake the body, anger that could not burst out in yelling or hitting, tears that could not be shed. If someone has done you wrong there may be unexpressed anger. We may postpone its release until the time seems appropriate, but meanwhile it must be stored in the body, and such storage creates a rigidity in the muscles, which in turn alters the normal distribution of energy. Over a lifetime, a huge accumulation of unfelt feelings may be stored and waiting for discharge.

The worst of it is that by limiting the expression of such feelings as hurt, anger, fear and sorrow, our ability to experience pleasure is also restricted. Pleasure is experienced in the expansive flow of energy through the body. This can't happen fully when major muscle groups are held permanently in contraction. You can't be happy if you won't be sad, and you can't be truly loving if you can't also be angry.

Managing emotions is improved by understanding the intimate connection between mind, body, energy, feelings, thoughts and action. The rest of this chapter will explore three useful ways of handling difficult emotions:

- *Emotional release*—discharging excesses of feelings safely out of range of other people.
- *Focusing*—exploring and analysing what's going on below the surface.
- *Communication of feelings*—using your emotional energy to create positive change.

EMOTIONAL RELEASE

In the previous section, Bodymind, we saw how the body can accumulate muscle tension from unreleased emotions.

If the backlog of emotional material builds up enough, the body may break down physically. Many doctors now acknowledge that physical illnesses have a psychological component. Heart attacks, strokes, cancer, even the common cold may well be responses to emotional overload. Modern cancer treatments include examining the person's inability to express anger. More doctors and health workers now pursue such additional treatments inspired by people such as John Harrison (*Love Your Disease, It's Making You Healthy*) and Louise Hay (*You Can Heal Your Life*). John Harrison[2] says: 'If . . . emotions are not dealt with, that is, expressed and forgotten, a chronic state of fear (anxiety), sadness (depression) or anger (aggression) may result. The long-term effect on the heart is disease.' Louise Hay[3] closely relates physical symptoms to emotional disturbances. She suggests for example that complete recovery from a heart condition may require the patient to look at how joy is blocked in their lives. Injuries to the feet and ankles can occur 'by accident' at times when the person feels they are lacking mobility and direction.

The greater the accumulation of suppressed feelings from the past, the more out of touch with the present we become. It's as if our mental computer is on overload and can't take an accurate reading. If too much anger is stored, the slightest incident becomes an excuse to discharge some of the excess. Some poor, unsuspecting sales assistant can become the dumping ground for rage unprocessed for twenty years. Grief inadequately acknowledged twenty years ago is held in the body and can cast a cloud of depression over whatever is happening now.

Unfortunately, some of us mistakenly think that by preventing tears we stop grief, or by holding our tongues we stop anger. We may stop the emotion from coming out, but it stores in our body awaiting a more appropriate time to manifest. We can choose what we do with an emotion, but we can't choose how *not* to have it. We can decide to find out more about the other person, or deepen our understanding of them to see if that changes the way we feel. But if it doesn't, then we would do better to acknowledge the emotion and decide how to deal with it practically.

A current problem may be triggering an old, repressed response. Letting it all out on another person is inappropriate. Even without a backlog, it is not always best to say all you feel. If you don't want to carry around the unexpressed feelings, you may want to let them go at some other time and place.

The discharge of excess feelings can occur during normal daily activity. Travelling to and from work, gardening and housework are splendid opportunities for digesting our experiences—there's more to walking the dog than meets the eye! We also discharge some of our pent up feelings nightly in our dreams. Meditation, too, can be a useful tool.

Do you need to release pent up feelings?

People release anger by talking things over with friends, playing sport, going for a run, screaming in the car, breaking pencils, ripping old telephone books, or doing specific bioenergetic exercises.[4]

To do these exercises you need a quiet place where you will be alone and not overheard. You can express your angry feelings while you rhythmically hit a mattress, or throw pillows around the room, or wring a towel. Much of our anger is locked in shoulder muscles, upper arms and fingers. Such exercises give the body a chance to release this muscle tension. Let yourself make noises— much tension is locked in the throat. If you start on one feeling, others may also come out. Give your body a chance to shake or cry if that's what you need. Of course, stop yourself if you feel too overwhelmed.

Releasing pent up feelings should be a relief. However, if you feel drained, you may not be quite ready to let go completely. Counsellors who include body work and bioenergetics in their approach can sometimes help when problems seem out of proportion. Programs will include exercise, massage, controlled pressure and gentle touching to release contracted muscles. Homeopaths, chiropractors, health food shops, New Age bookshops, or magazines can refer you to a therapist who uses these techniques. Enquiries should find you one in most cities and towns.

FOCUSING

By far the best thing you can do with a difficult emotion is feel it, explore it and get to the bottom of it.

By focusing we mean here the art of concentrating on a problem with a through-the-body approach until the problem unravels in your consciousness. It also means paying attention to energy flows and body awareness—attending to what is not yet clearly understood. You can use this focusing method for business and personal problems, and to increase creativity. It changes the way you deal with conflict.

To focus well, you need to grasp two basic concepts. Eugene Gendlin, in his valuable book *Focusing*, calls these *felt sense* and *body shift*.

Felt Sense

The same kind of perception that lets you know you have just touched something, or you are lying in a particular position in bed, or you have pulled a muscle in your back, can also give you a great deal of other information. With this *kinaesthetic* awareness (body awareness) you will feel very subtle muscular responses and energy flows. This is your bodymind computer registering everything that is going on. Take a moment now to feel energy in your body. Put down the book and shake your hands vigorously for about thirty seconds, then hold them out in front of you. You should feel energy streaming through your fingertips, though energy flows are usually more subtle than this.

Bodymind—your miraculous computer.

Most people know about anxiety churning the stomach, pain in the chest from hurt feelings, the dry mouth and tight solar plexis of great fear. These kinaesthetic perceptions are ones we need to be in tune with to define our feelings clearly. It has been argued that the body awareness *is* the feeling.

A felt sense may be as clear and precise as the body awarenesses we have described above, but usually it is a fuzzier and broader sensation because it includes much more information than just feeling. We believe we think with our heads, but in truth we know about a lot of things via the body and the energy flowing through and surrounding the body. Is it demonstrable? Try these exercises. You'll find the contrasts help you pinpoint each felt sense.

1. Think for a moment about your mother. Don't go into details about her eyes, or the last time you saw her, or whether she's alive or dead. Just tune into yourself and into the general sense of 'all about my mother'.

When you have some sense of that, switch to thinking 'all about my father'. See if you can collect some kinaesthetic information about the contrast between the sense of 'all about mother' and 'all about father.'

If you could feel the difference between the two experiences you now know where to look. 'All about mother' was the *felt sense* about mother. The sensation you got with 'all about father' was the *felt sense* about father.

If you were not aware of a difference between the two felt senses, you were probably trying to *think* it out, using your head instead of your body sense. Try another comparison.

2. Close your eyes and tune into someone you particularly like. Imagine yourself having a good conversation with them, then imagine that someone you don't like much walks in and joins the conversation. The first felt sense was about a conversation with one person. When you imagined the second person joining in, did you sense yourself shutting down, becoming tight in places? The second felt sense concerned a good conversation interrupted by someone you didn't really like. Many individual pieces of information make up these

two experiences, yet you know all about them in an instant, such is the sophistication of our 'awareness computer'. All the information is given to you at once without the thousands of verbal labels that would so clutter your consciousness you'd probably blow a fuse.

3. Whether or not you have succeeded in locating where a felt sense occurs, try one more contrast and focus particularly on what's going on in your muscles.

Imagine you are playing a game of tennis and you are about to serve the ball. When that is clear, switch to imagining yourself playing golf and about to drive the ball for that game. The thousands of pieces of information about how to hold your body for each shot are contained in an instant of through-the-body awareness.

4. Now focus for a moment on some difficulty, big or small, you are having. It might be an impossible boss or a piece of equipment that frustrates you. When your felt sense is established, change your focus to another sort of problem—a difficulty with someone you live with, or what you will cook for dinner.

This is a much harder exercise than the previous three and the felt sense may not be quite as clear. The more troubling the problem or the conflict, the *easier* it is to get in contact with its felt sense. It's troubling you precisely because you are in contact with its felt sense.

To understand the process of focusing there is one more concept to explain.

Body Shift

Unravelling a problem releases energy.

This is a release of energy in the body that occurs when you remember or label accurately for the first time something that is hard to bring to conscious mind.

You've had the experience of this energy release many times in your life but, as with 'felt sense', you've probably never talked about it or given it a name.

Have you ever had to wait to get a word into a conversation? Then, when the moment comes, you realise you have forgotten what it is you wanted to say? You feel considerable relief when you recall at last what it was you wanted to say. That relief is a *body shift*.

Do you remember what it's like when you leave the house without something you intended to take? You know you've forgotten something but you can't think what. You rack your brains. Was it something for work? Something you needed at lunch-time? Perhaps if you let it rest, then suddenly the thought just appears. It might be of the order of 'I was going to take in the photos of my last holiday for Bill to see', or 'I forgot to lock the back door'. When you remember, it can be too late, but it's still a relief to know what it is. You'll probably move in the seat (if you are sitting) in response to your energy burst.

A similar relief and release of energy occurs any time you tune into the felt sense of something that is troubling you and up pops a new set of words describing exactly what is the matter. The accurate labelling undoes a knot inside you and you relax. Your label might be: 'The main thing about it is that I feel he doesn't respect me.'

This unknotting does not occur when you just think about the problem the same old way. The same old way may include variations on: 'Aren't they awful?' or 'I'm so terrible.' Body shifts, which are real changes, come from a through-the-body approach, not a mind approach. They bring a new insight or understanding. Now that we have identified a felt sense and a body shift, let's look at the actual process of focusing—the concentration on a problem or conflict. First, it requires a little preparation of your space.

Whether you focus alone or with someone else, it is best done quietly and comfortably, sitting somewhere you won't be interrupted. But expert focusers do it everywhere—walking along the street, on public transport, having a shower.

The Focusing Process

The task is to focus on the felt sense and ask yourself at least one of these questions: 'What's the main thing in this?', 'What's the crux of this?', or 'What's most important here?' or 'What's really the matter?' and then, *without* answering yourself, *stop, listen and wait.*

Use focusing to find the core of the problem.

After a few moments some labels for the essence of the problem will pop into your mind. Now you're really listening to the part of yourself that senses the whole problem but has not yet made it conscious. As you get your labels right it's a bit like untangling knotted fishing line. As the next piece gets an accurate label you are able to advance on the tangled ball, which diminishes as you unravel each snarl.

If the problem is complex or otherwise hard to think about, you might find you have trouble focusing. Don't push across such barriers—use them. If you feel empty or overwhelmed, focus on what it feels like to be empty or overwhelmed by this difficulty. The result might be 'sad' or 'too much'. Whatever you do come up with, check back with the sensation again to confirm.

You may not be able to solve the whole problem in one session of focusing. You can promise yourself to revisit the problem soon. Some problems are so complex they can take months or years to untangle completely. You don't need to find all the answers today— live with the question. Be open to any helpful insight or information. Certain problems demand more inner strength than we presently have. They may require finishing a relationship, risking a change in jobs, or setting firm limits, and we may not be ready yet. We need to respect our own unfolding process and not be too harsh on ourselves.

Likewise, we need to respect another person's unfolding. Have you ever felt irritated by someone who is spending a lot of energy on what seems a relatively minor issue? Perhaps it's deciding whether or not to see an ex-boyfriend or ex-girlfriend, how to ask the boss for some time off, or how to behave at a party. We're more tolerant of a child needing time to figure something out, but not nearly as tolerant of an adult taking time over something that wouldn't be an issue for us. If you know how to focus for yourself, you might show someone else how to explore this way. At least it will give you more patience with them. We're all dealing with our own knotted fishing line of unconscious, unprocessed data. What is important is the process of untangling, labelling, making conscious, and that's what we acknowledge when we attend to someone's problem patiently.

Magnification

When you use a telescope, a microscope or a camera zoom lens, you magnify an image, making clearer and larger a smaller part of an object, be it a galaxy, an atom or a landscape.

Once you have focused on the problem and come up with a label for the crux of the matter you magnify it. Then you ask yourself, 'Now, what's the main thing in this?' Focusing may not *solve* a problem—it is concerned with *identifying* it.

Steps to Focusing

If you have a problem dealing with someone who telephones you too frequently, try these steps:

Step 1: Relax.

Step 2: Feel for the problem—you need a felt sense of 'All about the problem I have with the too-frequent telephone calls'.

Step 3: Get to the core—ask yourself what's the main problem? The answer might be: 'They're making demands of me when I want to get on with other things.'

Step 4: Check back with the felt sense. If the words and felt sense don't quite match, you will feel discomfort and need to repeat Step 3. Although others' demands are part of the problem, it may not be the core of it.

Repeating Step 3 might produce 'I do want their friendship, but my attention is elsewhere and when I talk I sound distracted and I'm worried they are offended.' If this label is right, a small energy release may confirm it.

Step 5: When you have gone back and forth between Steps 3 and 4 until the felt sense and the label match, a body shift will signal your success. It may be just a sigh, the relaxing of a tight facial muscle or your resettlement in a chair. You might even feel hot or goosebumpy all over—energy held by the tension is discharging. Encourage the shift—let yourself sigh, allow your body to reposition. Give yourself a minute to feel normal again and then perhaps go into another round—increase the magnification. If your fundamental problem at the end of the first round is that you don't want to offend your telephone-addicted friend, focus now on this: 'What's the main reason for not wanting to offend them?' Off you go again, listening to the felt sense, waiting for a label to pop up, comparing that label with the felt sense, and continuing the enquiry until you find the label that is just right.

How Does Focusing Help?

Every time we have to work out a problem or difficulty by looking inside ourselves to discover what's going on, we are focusing. An insight might come in the shower, or when driving along in the car last thing at night or first thing in the morning—moments when our conscious mind has 'slipped out of gear into neutral'. As we explore the issue, empathy with the other person often grows of its own accord. The problem ceases being 'their fault' and becomes our own evolving journey. Our self-understanding speeds up when we take time to tune in to the felt sense. Whenever emotions are high or we are confused or uncertain of our own feelings, focusing is a great help.

COMMUNICATION OF FEELINGS

The most obvious way to release emotions is by expressing them to the people directly involved. We've realised that we may first need to release some excess of feeling before we start. We may also need to use focusing to determine what's really going on. Much of what we feel can most fruitfully be brought up in conversation. But it depends how this is done, and for what purpose.

Anger, hostility, resentment and frustration can easily become destructive forces. But these emotions, often supposed negative, can become fires for positive change if you use their heat wisely. For example, your anger about a communication breakdown can be channelled into establishing a better system for messages. The following questions and goals help good self-management:

Why am I feeling this? What triggered your response? What did someone do? Have they touched on a sensitive issue?

Use anger as a fire for change.

What do I want to change? Your emotions tell you what you do and don't want, so use them to create change. What change do you want? Unfortunately, emotions are often misused to prove the other person wrong and hold grudges.

What do I need to let go of this feeling? Once people get hold of an emotion they sometimes have trouble finishing with it. If George makes you angry, you can stay angry, and if a difficult confrontation has hurt your feelings, you might stay hurt. Emotions should do their work and then pass through. It's not good to store up resentment. What will help you let go? Do you just need to explain yourself? Do you need an apology? Do you need to see someone making an effort?

Whose problem is this, really? How much is mine? How much is theirs? You may be angry that your teenage son's room is untidy. If you have to find something in there, then it's your problem. As it is your son's room, it's largely his problem. If your spouse spends all evening on the phone chatting to friends, it's your problem if you are missing the companionship. It's his problem if he's not getting done the other tasks he has set himself. If someone isn't doing something the way you'd like, whose problem is it? You will handle your communication more effectively if you are assertive about your problem but do no more than offer occasional suggestions about theirs. Where the distinction of which problem belongs to which person is blurred, one person is likely to interfere excessively. It is a common marriage problem to have one partner taking an inappropriate level of responsibility for the way the other person is living their life. Such blurred distinctions are often the source of difficulty that manifests itself in nagging.

What is the unspoken message I infer from the situation? Is it 'they don't like me'? or 'They don't respect me'? The conclusions we draw about someone else's behaviour are often the triggers for our excessive emotional reactions. If someone is abrupt with you, you might assume that they don't think you're worthy of their attention. If someone walks out and slams the door you may assume that they don't love you any more. Knowing how you interpret the unspoken message gives you a chance to vet that response and decide how realistic it is.

There are five goals worth bearing in mind whenever you decide to say what's going on for you:

1. *Aim to avoid the desire to punish or blame.* Take responsibility for how you feel. If you plan action, check that it is not vindictive. Are you blaming someone for your feelings? People do what they do, we respond how we do. There's a subtle but important difference between 'You make me mad' and 'When you do that, I get mad.'

2. *Aim to improve the situation.* High emotions indicate where change is wanted. Be sure you are going to make it better.

3. *Aim to communicate your feelings appropriately.* If something hurts you or angers you, you have a right to say so. Bottling it up jeopardises the relationship, but watch that you express yourself so that you know you would not become defensive if it was said to you. A well-chosen statement is invaluable for expressing anger and hurt (see Chapter 4, Appropriate Assertiveness).

4. *Aim to improve the relationship and increase communication.* People don't know you until they know how you feel. When talking about your good and bad feelings you are offering something immensely precious to the other person—the opportunity to know you. When someone tells you about their feelings they offer you the same gift. Treat them with care.

5. *Aim to avoid repeating the same situation.* If someone doesn't ring when they say they will, you may well feel worried or hurt. Managing your emotions also involves making sure that the situation won't recur. Explain your situation; say what you find difficult; ask to be treated in a particular way; fix the problem. This way you're looking after yourself and, in so doing, preserving the relationship.

Coping with Difficult Emotions in Others

Respect the communication of feelings. When someone is highly emotional, it's important to respect any communication of feelings. It's often very hard for people to talk about how they feel. It's easy to seal up the well by trying to dampen the other person or by not acknowledging their emotions. Jim wondered why his daughter never discussed her boyfriends with him until he realised how often he jumped in with advice or told her what she was doing wrong whenever she began to open up.

Be tolerant when others discharge emotions. It's a sign of maturity when you can allow some leeway for others to discharge their pent up emotions without taking offence or being caught up in them. Try active listening (see Chapter 2, Empathy) when someone is very emotional.

Reward behaviour that you do want.

Reward the behaviour you do want. Have you ever been annoyed by someone seeking attention? They might have been boasting, showing off, making repeated requests or talking excessively. It's easy to react negatively. Be aware that reminding and punishing as well as praising and even just noticing behaviour will reward attention-seekers. Behaviourally, whatever you reward you get more of. So reward behaviour you *do* want. Support their involvement and contribution and ignore their bids for attention, where possible.

Disengage from power struggles. People often use power to build their own self-esteem. It also can make you wild if their ability doesn't match their position, or if they test you with confrontations such as 'You can't make me.' Disengage from this kind of power struggle as soon as you recognise it. Fighting and giving in both reward negative behaviour. Support the other's sense of self-worth for reasons other than their ability to defeat you.

Don't retaliate. One of the most difficult emotions to handle is other people's desire for revenge, especially when you are the target. It springs from deep hurt sometimes. You may be able to tone it down if you pursue the issues of justice and fairness with them. Try to avoid feeling hurt, and try not to retaliate. You need to build trust. Consider how you can best convince the person that you respect their needs.

Avoid nagging and criticism. Have you ever been driven mad by someone who acts helpless for no good reason? The child who plays dumb to avoid helping with a dinner; the co-worker who pretends to be stupid so he won't get an extra task; the woman who plays dumb under the mistaken belief that it's feminine and appealing; the depressed person who maintains they are good for nothing, and that no one could ever love them or employ them.

We all need a certain amount of self-doubt—it's healthy. But we're talking here about self-doubt caused by deep discouragement as well as the self-doubting statements that have the effect of manipulating others. Criticism and nagging rarely help anyone. You can help by encouraging any positive attempts they make, however small. Focus on whatever is going right—don't dwell on pity or agree that nothing can change. Don't give up, although the way through for the other person may be a slow process of self-improvement, step by step.

Here are some useful tactics to support their underlying need for self-esteem, a sense of belonging, significance and identity.

- *Self-esteem*—Praise whatever is praiseworthy—often.

- *Feelings of significance*—Point out some of their special qualities. Include and repeat their options.

- *Sense of identity*—Support the ways they like to be different that don't hurt anyone else. Help them define personal territory, such as their own room, desk or filing tray. Communicate about matters specific to their interests.

- *Sense of belonging*—Openly value their contribution to, and their importance in, the group, family or team. Perhaps acknowledge your love or respect for them.[6]

Support basic needs for self-esteem, a sense of significance, identity and belonging.

SUMMARY

1. Don't indulge or deny—build richer relationships.
2. Emotions are body-mind and energy events.
3. Do you need to release pent up feelings?
4. Try focusing to find the crux of the problem.
5. Anger is a fire for positive change if you use its heat wisely.
6. To cope with difficult emotions in others, try active listening and support their need for self-esteem, significance and identity, and their need to belong.

Five questions to ask when angry/hurt/frightened

1. Why am I feeling so angry/hurt/frightened?

. . . .

. . . .

2. What do I want to change?

. . . .

. . . .

3. What do I need in order to let go of this feeling?

. . . .

. . . .

4. Whose problem is this, really? How much is mine? How much is theirs?

. . . .

. . . .

5. What is the 'message' I infer from the situation? (e.g. They don't like me? They don't respect me?)

. . . .

. . . .

Five goals to pursue for communicating emotions

1. Aim to avoid the desire to punish or blame.

Action? . . . .

. . . .

2. Aim to improve the situation.

Action? . . . .

. . . .

3. Aim to communicate your feelings appropriately.

Action? . . . .

. . . .

4. Aim to improve the relationship and increase communication.

Action? . . . .

. . . .

5. Aim to avoid repeating the same situation.

Action? . . . .

. . . .

If communication is not appropriate, what other action can I take?

. . . .

. . . .

NOTES

1. See Alexander Lowen, MD, *Bioenergetics* (New York: Coward, McCann and Geoghegan, 1975) and Ken Dychtwald, *Body-Mind* (USA: Jove, 1977).
2. John Harrison, *Love Your Disease: It's Keeping You Healthy* (Sydney: Angus & Robertson, 1984), p. 141.
3. Louise Hay, *You Can Heal Your Life* (California: Hay House, 1984).
4. Alexander Lowen, MD, and Leslie Lowen, *The Way to Vibrant Health— A Manual of Bioenergetic Exercises* (US: Harper Colophon Books, 1977).
5. Eugene Gendlin, *Focusing* (US: Everest House, 1978).
6. Rudolf Dreikurs and Vicki Soltz, *Children: The Challenge* (New York: Hawthorn, 1964).

CHAPTER SEVEN

Willingness to Resolve

Willingness to resolve is a key factor in conflict resolution. Indeed, sometimes it is all you need—where there's a will there's a way. Being willing and helping others to become willing to resolve is often a considerable challenge.

Can you remember a time when you were so hurt, angry or resentful that you didn't want to fix the problem? Is there someone in your life right now who angers you but you haven't sorted out why, or taken steps to fix the problem? Can you recall a situation like that from the past—if so, where?

What stops people from wanting to resolve a conflict? Are any of these relevant to your situation:

The unfairness
Self-respect/pride
Need for apology
Desire for revenge
Hurt
Anger
Resentment
'I was right, you were wrong'

Secondary Gains From the Conflict

What's the pay-off for hanging on to the problem?

Does hanging on to the problem have any benefits or advantages? It *may* be traumatic for you and for the other person to confront the real issue. There's a certain satisfaction in staying angry with someone whose values you deeply disagree with. Sometimes we define our values by the people and issues we oppose. When you've been deeply hurt by someone, you can also feel angry with them. Hurt and anger are often two sides of the coin. Just because anger is unexpressed doesn't mean it's not present. It shows up as spite or resentment. Both are forms of frozen anger—and this icy condition can be preserved for ages. There are people who have refused to speak to each other for twenty years because each is rigid with resentment. Many people know how to nurse grudges and resentment but don't know how to wipe the scorecard clean. When you hurt deeply it is often because someone has struck a blow to your self-esteem. You may need to defend the attack with justification and self-righteous indignation, but you might choose to reaffirm your belief in yourself and see them as mistaken rather than malicious.

When you don't forgive someone you don't have to consider the whole person. We tend to over-simplify by pigeonholing people as 'baddies' and 'goodies'. If we acknowledge the other person's full range we might also be faced with acknowledging our own bad points.

Sometimes it's difficult to admit that we, too, have a part in the conflict, and have put some logs on the fire. No matter how right we think we are, or how terrible they seem, we are part of the scene. To become willing to fix the problem, we have to change something inside us.

We may have to refocus priorities. How important is being right compared with resolving the problem?

Of course, being willing to *resolve* a problem does not mean you aren't in the right. It means you give up making the other person wrong, by wiping the slate clean and making a fresh start with each other. It means recognising the greater happiness flowing from having good relationships than from proving your point. You might choose to give up searching for evidence or for other people to agree with you, and simply say how you feel. Use 'I' statements. You can start the ball rolling by distinguishing between self-righteousness and integrity.

Would you rather be right or happy?

Deciding to resolve a problem can require a major internal shift. We sometimes hold onto a grudge for some secondary gain—the

EVELYN'S STORY

I was furious. Last Saturday my boyfriend arrived two hours late for a date, without any excuse. He hadn't rung—he seemed to think it was just fine to treat me that way. I was livid, and screamed at him to get out. He left all right, in a hurry. I think he was amazed at my reaction. I haven't spoken to him for a week. Until this morning, I was still festering. Today I realised how unwilling I was to resolve the problem. While I was gardening, I applied the pay-off test, asking myself 'What benefit is there for me in not

forgiving him? I am very unwilling to resolve.' The truth came to me surprisingly quickly: I had wanted to break off the relationship for months and hadn't known how to. I'd put it off because I felt guilty about it. Now that he was so definitely at fault, I wasn't going through the breaking-up process, nor did I have to feel guilty. When I realised all this, I felt if I left it like this it would be very dishonest. I owe it to him and myself to finish it off more considerately and responsibly.

pay-off. Willingness to resolve something begins with a quiet moment in which to explore the pay-off for *not* resolving it, and to assess the temptation to leave the problem as it is.

For things to change, first I must change.

Ultimately, both parties need to open up. But we cannot always directly influence someone else. We can look at our own unwillingess to resolve the problem without depending on the other person's willingness. As long as we say 'I can't let go until they do', we are not willing to resolve. Two people locked in resentment are locked into each other emotionally and energetically. If we release our own side, the other person may feel much freer to move than before. For things to change first I must change.

Your forgiveness frees you.

You don't have to let go with the other person present. Forgiveness is really up to you alone. Whether the other person is physically present or not, we are still connected. We're all swimming in the same psychic soup where each individual's thoughts and feelings add to the flavour. Alter an ingredient and it tastes different. Your changes free others to change. But, most important, your forgiveness frees you.

RICHARD'S STORY

I emigrated to Australia mostly, I'm afraid, to escape from an impossible relationship with my mother. Over the years we had shared fierce scenes and bitter feelings. For twelve months we had not even spoken to each other. I was the second son in the family and had not been nearly as clever at school as my older brother had. I felt my mother always compared me with my brother and that I, the second son, was second best in her book. One day, in a personal development workshop I unlocked some of my resentment about my mother. It was a very significant release for me. I arrived home late that night. Within minutes my mother phoned from England. She had been trying to reach me for some hours. She was ready to talk again and my insights helped me to accept the love she was trying to offer. Why did she ring just then? She had intuitively responded almost immediately to the shift I'd made. It gave me insight into the way things can change when I change.

What Does it Take to be Willing to Resolve?

It is often very hard to forgive someone who has hurt you badly. Sometimes people who have been deeply hurt prefer to arrive at forgiveness in slower stages. For example, they might recognise that they are open to the idea of forgiveness—but are not yet ready to take this step. This is enough to begin the process of unlocking the problem. Consider the actions you are willing to take, no matter how small, to open up or change the situation.

Have you ever noticed how a particular person or characteristic really irritates you? Have you noticed that it doesn't really irritate others? Have you watched someone get really irritated by something that simply doesn't bother you, and you wonder what all the fuss is about? This is because our view of anything or anyone is seldom neutral. We look through 'coloured glasses', and some of the colours are shoulds and shouldn'ts; rights and wrongs; likes and dislikes; past experiences and upbringing. Ask yourself which 'coloured glasses' you are looking through.

Which 'coloured glasses' are you looking through?

Sometimes our views and reactions are filtered through some pain or anger deep inside us so we keep bringing up the same issue over and over again.

It's easier to see when others' reactions are more extreme than

ROSEMARY'S STORY

I was so hurt by my husband's infidelity that I really wasn't willing to forgive him. His betrayal of our marriage just welled up and festered inside me. But, after a while, my feelings changed just a little and I realised that I was willing to become willing to forgive him. This was a first step which, once I realised it, was enough for me to open up to change.

the situation calls for. When you're the one who's hopping mad, it all feels perfectly justified.

There may be someone in the office who talks a great deal about themselves. Others in the office, not influenced by unconscious prejudices, may simply think: 'There goes G. showing off again. I wonder why she needs to do that?' They disapprove and may even express their strong dislike but they are not so emotionally engaged. But a person who grew up under the shadow of a more attractive and outgoing sister may find the situation throws up unresolved jealousies. Their reaction to the office chatterbox will be 'I can't stand how G. behaves.' The situation inflames them rather than informs them. This is a useful rule of thumb.

Are you informed or inflamed?

When a situation *informs* you, you only have the difficulty itself to deal with, but when it *inflames* you, there is more going on than meets the eye. When you are inflamed, you have work to do on yourself before changing anything else. There's a pair of coloured glasses you'd better take off and examine. When someone makes you angry, this anger tells you as much about *you* as about them. The point is why you respond that way! The more someone irritates you, the more you know you have something to learn about yourself from that person.

In particular, you will need to see where your willingness to resolve is interfered with by unconscious projection.

PROJECTION

Projection occurs when our own unconscious thoughts and feelings seem to be in the minds and behaviour of others, not in ourselves. We push something out of our awareness and see it, instead, coming from others. Projection is highly influential in our lives.[1]

Some psychologists find it useful to work with the idea that our personality is a complete package of human characteristics with positives and negatives, good and bad points—the full spectrum of human potential. Our upbringing allows us to be conscious only of a part of who we really are. The psychologist Carl Jung used the word *persona* to describe these conscious aspects of personality. Whether these aspects are good or bad, the significant point about the persona is that it is *known* to the person. It includes things that we accept are true about themselves. The persona is our self-image.

Jung used the term *shadow* to describe the unconscious side of who we are—our unconscious desires, wants, feelings, intentions or beliefs. It is the potential that has not unfolded: aspects of ourselves that we are not ready to know about; and emotional responses too

Is my shadow speaking?

painful to fully experience. It also includes the opposites of all our conscious wants or dislikes, as well as abilities or talents we are not ready to accept or express.

Few of us acknowledge all the bad things about ourselves, or have enough self-esteem to acknowledge all the good. Positive or negative when unacceptable, they become the shadow side of our personality. For instance, if anger, hatred, jealousy, or destructiveness are unexpressed and unresolved, wherever we go they follow us around just like our shadow.

Indirect anger can work like this: we 'accidentally' spill tea over the person we are angry with; or we inadvertently say how we hate red on a day that they wear red. Others are often much more aware of our repressed feelings than we are. We often have a very misleading self-image. We think we are kindly while we can be unconsciously very cruel. There's a rascal in all of us. It's a much less dangerous rascal when taken out and acknowledged alongside our other caring and law-abiding qualities.

When you are inflamed rather than informed—look within. You are probably caught in a projection from your shadow. Consider the hook, the symptom and the projection.

The hook: the behaviour in the other person that is inflaming you, in itself a neutral event. Your projection gets caught on this hook.

The symptom: high emotions (usually variations on anger and hurt).

The projection: what can you become aware of in yourself (your shadow) that is causing your strong reaction? It's worth looking in three possible areas:

1. Suppressed needs. You don't recognise a need you want served, and then unreasonably blame the other person when they prevent you from fulfilling it. For example you are inflamed when someone doesn't give you help they promised. Is your need for support considerably greater than you've realised?

Perhaps you are inflamed because someone else takes the credit for work you have done. Are you underestimating your own need to be recognised? You may be deeply hurt when a friend pulls out of an activity you planned to do together. Are you denying your own need for companionship? When we are unaware of needs that underlie our behaviour, we are unreasonably inflamed when they are not supported.

2. Unresolved personal history. An event may trigger unresolved stress or anger from a similar event in the past. Here are some examples:

(a) You have to deal with someone who is abusing a child but you're so angry and punitive you miss some of the facts. Anyone would demand justice and protection for the child, but why are you so extremely distressed? Does the situation trigger memories of violence or abuse in your own childhood?

(b) Your boss criticises everyone's work. No-one likes it, but you become particularly anxious and depressed. Did you respond to criticism like that some time in the past? Does he remind you of a teacher who really had it in for you?

(c) You have watched people dying in war, in poverty, and now you violently hate a particular government.

(d) An intimate relationship breaks up and your distress and depression seem bottomless. Are you tapping into more than immediate grief? Abandonment by a parent through divorce or death would be something to look at. If you couldn't deal completely with the distress then, it is highly likely to resurface now.

It sometimes seems that life throws up the opportunity to complete the past while you handle the present.

3. Unacceptable qualities or characteristics.

Acknowledge projections:
1. Suppressed needs
2. Unresolved personal history
3. Unacceptable qualities.

The quality suppressed can seem negative or just unattainable. In Aesop's fable, the fox, who couldn't reach the grapes, gave up in disgust, saying that the grapes were sour anyway. That fox was projecting his disappointment at his own failure onto the grapes. Some examples:

(a) You are unreasonably irritated by other people who seem to be in love with themselves. Is rage in some measure due to the fact that you don't acknowledge your own beauty?

(b) You are critical of someone who flaunts their sexuality. Are you jealous? If so, what is that jealousy based on? Do you play down your own sexuality?

(c) You feel alienated from someone who frequently explodes in anger. You yourself would never let loose in such a fashion. Is it worth asking yourself how you deny or suppress your own anger?

(d) Someone speaks to you disrespectfully. You think your curt remark is fair and appropriate, but others say it is out of proportion. It's time to look within. Are you blind to your lack of respect for the other person? They may be much less unaware of it than you, and indeed it may have been the trigger for their rudeness in the first place. Some children react very aggressively to an adult's lack of respect for them and a vicious circle of child-adult projection can begin.

Fanaticism is fuelled by suppressing the negative. By not allowing themselves any reasonable and honest doubt, fanatics become highly intolerant of any opposing views.

Many situations of discomfort can present an opportunity to turn the spotlight of awareness on your shadow. Simply knowing what piece of projection is going on can change your willingness to resolve an issue where your anger has become a major obstacle. Try the following self-discovery exercise.

Choose three people whose relationship with you is not completely trouble-free.	Focus on one of their qualities or ways of behaving you find irritating or upsetting.	Focus on your reaction. How do you feel about these irritations? Write several words until you have just the right one.	Why do you feel this way? Give reasons that concern *you* rather than them. Focus on suppressed needs or unresolved personal history or unacceptable qualities.

Someone you work with:

_____

A person you live with or a close friend:

_____

A parent or child of yours:

_____

Circumstances: Personal Design or Fate?

We have seen how our unconscious state colours how we see other people, but it does more than this. It constantly affects and changes what is actually going on. Carl Jung says that when an inner situation is not made conscious, it happens outside us as fate. At more obvious levels, this mechanism can work like this:

- Our aloofness from our own feelings can disturb others, so they become very emotional around us.
- A person who can't show their own anger can often make others very angry.
- A person who is unaware that they act in a very superior way provokes other people into pulling them down a peg or two.

This unconscious behaviour provides hooks on which others hang their own projections.

> I do not like thee, Dr Fell
> The reason why I cannot tell
> But this I know and know full well
> I do not like thee, Dr Fell.

This old rhyme points out a fundamental truth: we respond constantly to people's shadow side. Mutually interlocking hooks can draw people together in both love or conflict. The task is to become conscious of this and free each other from the enmeshed qualities of the relationship.

Thought both precedes and creates the circumstances in our lives. You think 'I'll turn on the light switch' just before you get up and do it. Unconscious thought is just as busy creating form. We don't know it's hard at work, but it is! We create patterns—they don't just happen to us. Our 'fate' is drawn to us by our 'shadow'. If we let them, these patterns can control us. Someone who was battered in childhood often grows up and marries a physically violent partner. The boy who was browbeaten by his mother can end up working for a very difficult woman boss. Whenever we are unresolved, new situations are likely to occur, carrying elements similar to those of past situations. We grow when we bring to the present situation the greater power, wisdom and skill we have developed since the original situation. We redesign the patterns of the past when we respond to new situations more successfully than we did before.

Your thoughts draw the events of your life to you.

The circumstances we would most resist are often the very ones that we attract. It's as if the fear or dislike of something actually draws the event to us. In coming to terms with circumstances such as disgrace, a financial disaster, or a marriage breakdown, we grow by breaking down limiting beliefs—for example, 'I'm a success because I make a lot of money.' or 'I'd never manage on my own.'

What you resist is what you get.

Look for unacknowledged projection wherever there are undesirable circumstances or patterns of trouble in your life. The situation you see out there is telling you something about yourself. Although it is true that human beings do get caught up in a grander sweep of events than the personal dilemmas of their own lives, generally it is useful to presume you are a magnet attracting to you whatever you need for your development. Thought is your method for drawing these things to you. Conscious thought is out of your control. The more aware you are of your internal processes, the more you are able to direct your thoughts to draw to you whatever you consciously desire.

The situation you see gives you messages about yourself.

We can use conflict situations as a potent tool for developing

LIZ'S STORY

Recently I started an exciting new relationship. This man was pursuing me in a way I loved—ringing me often and telling me how much he wanted to see me. We started to get very close. Then, suddenly, things changed. He rang far less frequently and then it became up to me to say I wanted to see him. I no longer looked forward to his calls. I found myself being quite short and sarcastic in our conversations. To a friend in whom I confided I said, 'You can't trust men at all. They are all the same. They say things they don't mean.' When I looked back, I saw how my relationships had often made this sudden turn. I became angry about men. I'd really rather not bother with them at all.

Why was I so mad? What was I really feeling? Then I saw I was scared of being hurt and left, and remembered that I felt like this when I was a kid. I would become close to my father, and I'd want to be with him more, but then he'd go away and I'd feel it was not safe to love him. I could see now

that there was a pattern to my relationships with men: at the point when we'd become close, the change happened and the man withdrew suddenly. My unacknowledged fear was that if I became close I would be hurt or left. The fear was drawing the reality of hurt and rejection into my life. This was something new I had learned about myself.

Then I started to wonder why Joe had decided to withdraw. Maybe he wasn't doing it to me at all. Maybe he wasn't trying to hurt me—maybe he, too, was scared for whatever reasons and 'shadows' he had. Maybe he was scared I didn't want to hear from him?

I softened toward him and decided I was ready to try a different approach. Next time I felt myself wanting to withdraw I decided to tell the truth and say: 'It seems to me that you've been calling me less often. I find myself feeling hurt and scared that you don't really want to see me.' I was ready to tackle a hurdle I'd always baulked at before.

our consciousness. Whenever we are in conflict, it's worth weeding the garden of our own minds.

MANAGING OTHERS' UNWILLINGNESS TO RESOLVE CONFLICT

For smooth resolution to conflict both parties need to be willing to resolve. In this chapter we have discussed ways in which you can bring yourself to that state of mind. Frequently your greatest challenge will be to move the other person to that point too. Although you might understand that they have their own suppressed needs, unacknowledged personal history or unacceptable qualities, it will rarely be appropriate for you to point this out.

To get a better response provide a better stimulus.

Don't diagnose your boss. It's not part of the social contract you have with each other. You will need less confrontational methods to calm your boss's inflammation and to bring him or her to the negotiating table. You need a very special relationship for it to be acceptable to diagnose each other. Therefore consider these alternatives:

Correct your part of the problem

When someone else is projecting onto you, you are rarely entirely innocent. How are you hooking their projection? Are you irritating the other person? To clean up your own act it's always worth looking at what is behind someone's complaint about you. The important thing is to adjust what needs correcting while maintaining a sense of proportion. There is no value in lacerating yourself with guilt because you have upset them. The largest part of their inflammation is their problem—you're just correcting your piece of it.

Look at how you come across. Ask yourself these questions:

- How am I using my *power*? Do I disempower or empower them? Am I playing victim, persecutor or rescuer roles? Did I offer clean choices, or did I make threats?
- Did I manage my own *feelings* first? Is my own *shadow* in the way of resolution?
- Did I use *empathy* blockers? Did I really listen to them?
- Did I use 'charged' language or did I use 'clean' messages?

Look at where misinterpretation seems to have occurred.

- Did we misinterpret each others position, motives, requirements, values, feelings?
- How can I clarify the issues?
- Do I need help to do this? A *mediator*?

Try a positive statement as a *diffuser* during conflict, or a *re-opener*, when the dust has settled and the atmosphere is calmer. For example: 'I'd really like to clear this up, how about you?'

Discuss the advantages there are for all of you if you resolve the problem.

Remember, someone may be gaining more from keeping the problem alive than from solving it. If this seems the case, you may need to *distance yourself* from the problem and allow them the space to own what is theirs. This may or may not mean physically distancing yourself from them. Work towards your own resolution, whereby you disengage and find calm and acceptance by understanding that you are not responsible for another. If you have done all you can and they are still locked into their pain, remember, your forgiveness frees you.

SUMMARY

1. What is the pay-off for hanging on to the problem?
2. Would you rather be right or happy? Commit yourself to the resolution of the problem rather than to self-righteousness.

3. Your forgiveness frees you.
4. Are you informed or inflamed? What coloured glasses are you looking through?
5. Uncover your own suppressed needs, unresolved personal history and unacceptable qualities that you may project during conflict.
6. Your thoughts draw the events of your life to you. What you resist is what you get. Use troublesome circumstances to weed the garden of your own mind.
7. Be aware that the other person is also hooked in and ask yourself what you can do to help them. Consider:
   (i)   correcting your part of the problem
   (ii) how you come across
   (iii) whether misinterpretation has occurred
   (iv) discussing with the other person the advantages of resolution.

NOTES

1. For a more detailed explanation of projection, see:
   Ken Wilbur, *The Spectrum of Consciousness* (Wheaton: Quest, 1979).

ADDITIONAL READING

Peter O'Connor, *Understanding Jung, Understanding Yourself* (Sydney: Methuen, 1985).
Joseph Campbell (ed.), *The Portable Jung* (New York: Penguin, 1971).

CHAPTER EIGHT

Mapping the Conflict

Have you ever had a problem and felt like this?

- I'm confused. I can't work out what's really going on.
- I'm stuck. There seems no way out of the problem.
- There are too many factors involved. Where do I start?
- Something else was going on, but I don't know what it was.
- The situation is hopeless—it's a personality clash.
- How inconsiderate! How could somebody behave like that?

It's moments like these you need . . . *maps*. Maps give a clear picture, show how things relate to each other, and show you things you may not otherwise see. So before moving into action to solve a conflict, create your map. You can do it alone, alongside a special friend, with others involved in the conflict, and especially in problem-solving meetings.

Remember the story about the orange in Chapter 2 and the importance of *going back to needs* to find win/win solutions? This is what maps help us do. Their great value is in their orderly, systematic approach.

Step 1. What's the Problem?

Label the issue in broad terms. There is no need yet to focus on or analyse the nature of the problem. Where the issue is someone in the workplace who is not doing their fair share of the job, the label you might write down is 'workload division'. Where there are personality clashes and communication has deteriorated, the label could be 'communication'. At home, where the problem is who does the washing up or the kids are not keeping their rooms tidy, perhaps label the issue 'washing up' or 'household chores'. Don't get anxious about whether or not it is exactly right, simply get down the nature of the area or topic to be mapped. Don't define the problem in terms proposing a yes/no, either/or choice. Keep the problem definition open-ended.

Define the issue in a general statement.

WHO: ....

NEEDS: ....

....

WHO: ....   FEARS: ....   WHO: ....

NEEDS: ....   NEEDS: ....

....

FEARS: ....   FEARS: ....

....   THE ISSUE   ....

....

....

WHO: ....   WHO: ....

NEEDS: ....   NEEDS: ....

....   WHO: ....

FEARS: ....   FEARS: ....

....   NEEDS: ....

....

FEARS: ....

....

Step 2. Who is Involved?

Identify the major parties involved.

Decide who the major parties are—you might list each individual (each member of a family or team), or whole teams, sections, groups or organisations (e.g. salesmen, receptionists, directors, clients, public, government). As long as the people involved share needs on the issue, they can be grouped together. A mixture of individual and group categories is fine too.

If you are mapping a new school policy on teacher-student ratios, the parties involved would be teachers, students, headmaster, the Education Department, parents and perhaps politicians and the media. An internal problem might involve only the first three groups.

If you map two people having a clash in an office, it may include Joan and Bob and the rest of the staff—or you may need to list everyone separately or include a supervisor.

Step 3. What Do They Really Want?

What are the needs?
What are the fears?

For each major party, you then list the significant *needs* and *fears* that are relevant to the issue. You clarify the motivations behind the issue. People are motivated by what they want and move toward, and what they don't want and move away from.

By mapping needs and concerns, we broaden the picture and the possible options for solutions to be addressed when the map is complete.

Needs

Use this term lightly—it could mean wants, values, interests or the things you care about. Simply ask the question: 'Around the issue of . . .' what are your/their major needs?' You may be asking it of yourself, of another person, or *about* another person or party. Needs might include: satisfying and secure work; respect; acknowledgment and understanding; a tidy house/desk; being allowed to make a mess; having everything legal and aboveboard.

Sometimes the same need applies to several or all groups. It can be worthwhile to repeat the need under each heading to reveal how much the people have in common.

Sometimes it's difficult for people to get off their solutions and go back to needs. You can lead them with questions like 'Your answer to the problem is to do X. What needs will be met?' Their reply to this is likely to be about their underlying needs. Occasionally mapping goes off at a tangent when another person starts talking about their problem in the midst of charting one person's needs and fears. You might complete their digression politely by extracting one of their needs or fears from what they are saying. This can then be charted on their place on the map. Continue by asking them whether it would be okay to return to where you originally were in the mapping process.

Fears

Fears are acknowledged by mapping.

These can be concerns, anxieties, worries. You do not have to debate whether or not the fear is realistic before it is listed. For example, you may have a fear about something your rational mind knows is very unlikely to happen, yet the fear still lurks underneath, wanting to be recognised. These are important to have on the map. One of the real benefits of mapping is the opportunity to air irrational fears and have them acknowledged on the map.

Fears might include:

- failure and loss of face
- doing the wrong thing
- financial insecurity

- being rejected, disliked, unloved
- loss of control
- loneliness
- being judged or criticised
- losing your job
- not enough income
- uninteresting work
- being ordered around
- paying too much
- having to start all over again

Use the fears category for drawing out motivations that don't surface so easily when considering needs: 'I need respect. I fear lack of respect.'

Listing the Right Needs and Fears

The most important thing to remember is to focus on the needs and fears of all parties until the map is complete. Don't be sidetracked into implications, 'what abouts?' or solutions. If the group persists in sidetracks, capture the issue on a separate piece of paper. Stick doggedly to: 'What are the needs? What are the fears?' You may have to sift out solutions being offered as needs. During the process of mapping smoking (see Map 1), the facilitator asked 'What do they need?' and the answer came back 'Timed breaks for everyone.' This was, in fact, a solution. The need behind it was something more like 'fair distribution of the workload'.

When someone makes a comment about something in the conflict that isn't working or makes them unhappy or dissatisfied, use your skill to find out what is behind the comment and reshape it as a need or fear. For example, a comment like 'Meetings are a waste of time. They go on and on', you could ask 'What do you need?' 'To spend less time in meetings.' You could also ask, 'What do you fear?'—'Not enough time to get my work done' This broadens the issue from what might otherwise be a digression on whether meetings go on too long or should go on at all. Keep to the whole picture of what people do and don't want out of meetings.

When you are trying to map the needs and fears of individuals and groups not present, it is essential to focus on what *they* would say their needs and concerns are. For example, your idea of a woman who's always late might be 'She needs to be on time'! What she herself needs may be something else—she may need a longer lunch-hour, more support with the kids, a new car that doesn't break down, or some help with time planning! Don't say: 'They need to be more understanding!' That statement is really about *your* need for more respect and acknowledgment. That's quite valid though. Put it down on your own list. Also, maybe there is something they need before

Handle digressions by charting the relevant need.

they can respect you more. They may need more communication or information from you. Of course, they may need more respect or acknowledgment, too. If you suddenly get an insight into what you need, consider the possibility that they need it too.

You Can Make a Map Any Time, Anywhere and With Anyone!

It is best to do your map on a large piece of paper. At a meeting clip butcher's paper onto an upright whiteboard and write with thick pens. Try to use several colours—one colour for the issue and the parties, another for needs, another for fears. Yet many a first class map has been made on a serviette in a restaurant with an old pencil!

Make a map quickly in your own head before starting a new job or living arrangement, planning a holiday with friends, making deals or agreements—any time in any personal or work relationship. You don't need to have a conflict for mapping—use it to prevent conflict. Maps can be used before drawing up a plan. For example, where a financial cutback is essential, a mapping exercise with all concerned can make a huge difference to implementing the cutbacks and to the attitudes of those concerned.

You can do a map by yourself. At times you'll only be guessing how it is for the other parties, but the process broadens your perspective. It will probably highlight some areas you want to know more about, which will give you some good questions to ask others about their needs before you head into solutions.

You can make a map with other people. You can initiate a mapping session in your work, home or any other group activities you are involved in. It's quite simple to say: 'Let's get a clear picture of the situation before we go further. Let's hear everyone's needs and concerns on this issue.' Maps can be productive with the following:

- Relationships.
- Preparations for business negotiations.
- Negotiations which have broken down (See Map 1).
- Custody arrangements and property divisions at the end of a marriage or de facto relationship.
- Teams or work areas where communications are difficult or there is a 'problem' person (See Map 3).
- Households.
- Advertising briefs.
- Factions not working well together (See Map 2).
- Planning meetings.
- Impending change. For example: Forming or carrying out new policies and regulations in large organisations.

Mapping addresses the future. You make maps so that you can come up with some real options. Use mapping for current situations, not those which are no longer negotiable, e.g. mapping an office no-smoking policy already in place is pointless, but some unresolved effects from the policy may need mapping. Perhaps non-smokers in the office are resentful of the length of time smokers take for their smoking breaks outside.

Stay on track with your map. If you find that you are sidetracking or that other issues are coming up, a second map may be required. While mapping the issue of smoking breaks, you may find environmental issues may emerge and also merit a map.

We often think that if we have obviously conflicting needs (for example, two people want the same promotion), then it is dangerous to make the clash visible. Not bringing a difficulty out into the open is usually far more risky than exposing it. Exposing the problem in terms of needs and concerns often helps new options emerge.

Clarify the legitimate needs behind a hidden agenda.

People who are considered 'very difficult' nevertheless have needs and fears that can be mapped—and the mapping will make you more able to deal with them. 'We have a personality clash' often really means 'I don't know what is making this person tick and my standard methods of dealing with people are not working.'

Go back to needs. You may well start receiving a totally different response from them once you have. There may be ways of meeting their needs that you haven't previously thought of, and your map might lead you to see new solutions. The crankiness of a teenager may be to mask a fear that they are not loved by the parent. Perhaps a special outing planned just for them might show them you really do care and fix a lot of other problems at the same time.

A lot of negativity from a fellow worker may be mapped as a frustrated need for recognition. You might address this with a compliment at the next staff meeting.

How to Read Your Map

- Look for new learnings and insights—things you hadn't seen or now find clearer. Mapping helps you see what it's like to be in the other person's shoes.
- Look for 'common ground'—similar needs or interests.
- Look for a common vision and build up what values and ideas are upheld by all. In Map 2, non-smokers listed 'not to have extra work', while smokers listed 'work flow to continue.' Both groups saw 'smooth work flow' as part of their common vision.
- Combine different values and perspectives. What values and ideas can be incorporated into a common vision because they matter to one of the parties? Footpaths which were cigarette butt-free mattered to the non-smokers and could readily be incorporated into the common vision by smokers too. Ideally, the common

vision should be broad enough to include the individual values of all the parties. For example, a parent cares about homework being done, while their child cares about having fun. The common vision should contain both homework *and* fun.

- Look for hidden agendas such as particular pay-offs for one party if a problem is solved one way and not another. A common unexposed pay-off is the desire to save face. Clarify the hidden agendas as additional needs and concerns on the map.
- Look for the areas of difficulty that most need attention.
- Look for leads. What didn't you know before that now seems to need following through?
- Build wins. Identify elements that would help someone else—especially concessions you could easily oblige with.
- Look for what it would take to make wins for all parties.

Design answers that incorporate wins for everyone.

Analyse these considerations yourself and with all the participants. Then list the points demanding attention. Now you are ready for the next stage—developing options (see Chapter 9 Designing Options).

The process of mapping has many benefits:

- It structures the conversation and usually keeps it away from excesses of emotion. People can lose their tempers any time but do tend to keep them toned down while mapping.
- It creates a group process so that the problem can be aired co-operatively.
- It provides a forum where people can say what they need.
- It builds empathy and acknowledges people who may not feel they were being understood before.
- It enables you to see both your own and other people's points of view much more clearly.
- It organises everyone's views on an issue.
- It points out new directions.

SUMMARY

There are three steps to mapping:

STEP 1: Define the issue in a general statement.

STEP 2: Name the major parties involved.

STEP 3: What are the needs and fears of each person or group involved?

Use maps alone, with a friend, with your conflict partner and with groups of people. Analyse your map for new insights, common ground, and a common vision. Focus on key issues and identify elements on which to build the win/win. Then move to designing new options.

MAP 1

A woman was unhappy because her neighbour wanted to build a high brick fence between their properties. The plan is about to go to Council for approval. She came to a Conflict Resolution course feeling very angry and helpless. She mapped the situation and left the workshop deciding to invite her neighbour in for a cup of tea and to get to know him a little, rather than fighting over the wall. She felt far less angry and helpless. The others in the course, who participated in the mapping, saw the value of mapping the needs, rather than immediately seeking a solution. They had started off siding strongly with the woman about how horrible the neighbour was, and making suggestions about how she could make it difficult for him. After the map they were much more concerned about the neighbour's fear and sense of isolation and about how the woman could help him and herself, too.

HER

NEEDS
—open space
—her property left intact
—to maintain her property value
—good communication and friendly
   relationship with her neighbour

FEARS
—feeling boxed in
—being walked over
—reprisal if he's knocked back by Council
—isolation
—paying toward something she didn't want
—having to look at a big brick wall

THE FENCE

HIM

NEEDS
—privacy
—security
—his dogs enclosed
—the neighbour's co-operation and
   communication

FEARS
—losing his dogs
—dogs being a nuisance to the neighbours
—burglary
—social contact he may not handle well

MAP 2

A policy of no-smoking in the building was introduced and some of the smokers began taking more frequent or lengthy breaks sometimes outside the building. The organisation was often divided into smoking and non-smoking camps. The staff in one section met to try and solve the difficulties. Mapping created a broader perspective on the issue. Non-smokers saw that smokers still had their addiction

SMOKERS

NEEDS
—adequate time for a smoke
—respect and communication
—place to smoke
—frequent breaks
—tolerance
—work flow to continue
—some need to work and smoke at the same time

FEARS
—not enough breaks
—animosity
—withdrawal symptoms
—discipline, sanction
—low opinion of others
—bad weather conditions

SMOKING BREAKS

NON-SMOKERS

NEEDS
—equality of breaks
—clean air in all areas—including building entrance
—no evidence of cigarettes
—smoke-free places for breaks and lunch
—stable, reliable workplace
—no extra work
—respect and communication
—telephones to be answered when people are absent

FEARS
—being taken advantage of
—disruption
—health deterioration
—being seen as petty and vindictive
—not being understood

MANAGEMENT

NEEDS
—efficiency
—healthy workforce
—good morale
—low level of conflict
—successful smoke-free zone model
—acceptance of the policy

FEARS
—compensation claims
—prosecution
—poor public image
—disruption and inefficiency
—poor morale

to deal with and the smokers saw that some of the non-smokers resented the number of breaks they took. Apathy and irritation was diminished once each point of view gained more respect and understanding. The debate and strong emotions over smoking versus non-smoking moved on to solving some of the remaining problems. Alternatives such as answering machines to take smokers' calls when they were absent, outside cigarette bins and separate eating areas with separate airconditioning units were amongst the suggestions considered.

MAP 3

A section supervisor felt very uncomfortable about confronting a receptionist who was taking so much time off that other staff members had to cover the reception area. The receptionist, a single mother, was often called away suddenly over difficulties with her three-year-old child. The supervisor, a reserved person, found it hard to handle the situation, and her hesitancy annoyed other section staff. A mapping exercise made the supervisor more confident about tackling the problem. Some of the options she went off to work with were:

- Hold a staff meeting and map the issue.
- Help the receptionist set her priorities. She herself could decide if it was appropriate for her to hold this job.
- Help the receptionist explore more reliable childcare options.
- Consider the reception work as a job-share position.
- Create a backup roster system with the staff so that relief would not be so random.

SECTION HEAD

NEEDS

—to have the work done
—to carry out her responsibilities and report to her supervisor
—to care about the receptionist and her personal life
—to nurture the people in her team
—to overcome her difficulty with being assertive
—to have her team happy and productive

FEARS

—loss of respect and status from above and from her team
—being 'bossy' or hard
—loss of control
—others will gang up and report her
—the other workers' anger and resentment
—upsetting the receptionist

COVERING RECEPTION

RECEPTIONIST

NEEDS

—to look after her child
—to have an income
—support as a single mum
—to cope as a mum and to show that she can
—respect
—acceptance in the team
—stability

FEARS

—job loss
—failure as a mother
—rejection
—discussing her situation and being seen as not coping
—loss of control
—stigma of being a single mum
—having her child reported as neglected

OTHER TEAM MEMBERS

NEEDS

—to fulfil their own roles without disruption
—to be respected for their skills and positions
—to show support and care for the receptionist but not at the expense of their own workload
—a receptionist they can rely on

FEARS

—the problem won't change or will get worse
—being manipulated
—having no choice to say 'no'
—feeling powerless
—being used
—being unsupported
—seen as inadequate in their own jobs because of not having enough time

CHAPTER NINE

Designing Options

Mapping has given you the opportunity to survey the terrain. Developing some new options for better solutions is the next logical step. Invite as many possibilities as you can. This is a creative process.

Good conflict resolvers are good at designing options, thinking spontaneously, breaking old habits and trying new ways. The creative process is like diving into a treasure trove of possibility. What you bring to the surface depends on what you are looking for. Look for solutions where everyone can win and you will probably find them.

Clearly defined win/win goals reduce power struggles and help the relationship. Power politicking takes place when people don't believe that the solutions will meet their needs. Even if the situation cannot fully support everyone involved, solutions that acknowledge the other person's needs say 'I care about you', 'I respect you' and 'You have the right to need what you need.'

There are three distinct stages:

- creating options
- choosing options
- acting on the chosen option

STAGE 1: Creating Options

Define the problem in terms of needs.

Define the problem in terms of needs. Once you are clear what everyone's needs are, open up the possibilities. You are trying to design an answer that incorporates a win for everyone and turns the protagonists into partners in the search for a solution. Is there any common ground where you both want similar things? Will the needs dovetail? For example, you need the car at 2 p.m. and I don't need it until 5 p.m.

What does the plan need for them to accept it? Does it need to include something that helps them save face? There may be someone behind the scenes who is pushing a particular point of view that must be acknowledged. There may be vital issues, yet to be discussed, that must be considered.

People feel more committed to solutions they have had a hand in developing. Try to involve others' suggestions, even if you have a perfectly good plan. They might be more enthusiastic about their plan than yours, even if it's the same plan. As well, use active listening to consider other people's suggestions.

Develop options together.

Use a Design Approach

Conflict resolution is not just made up of skills in active listening and assertiveness. It's also essential to design practical suggestions. Don't keep on yelling at the baby not to touch the vase. Move the vase until the baby is old enough to understand. If people at work keep on using a particular door as a short cut and it is annoying, lock the door and signpost an alternative route.

Be practical.

Think of an annoying persistent situation. Are any of these options relevant to designing new solutions?

Information and its Flow

Is decision-making blocked by lack of information? Is more commitment needed to pass on the information? What would help?

- More information needed? From where? Who should have it?
- More simply presented information, e.g. illustrations, summaries?
- Clarification?
- Earlier reporting?
- Regular times to talk?

Structure and Procedures

Do structures or procedures need to be updated? Consider:

- New lines of authority and responsibility.
- Updated report-back systems.
- Changed instructions.
- Introducing a formalised set of procedures.
- More planning.

Objects and Services

Are physical objects or available services part of the solution? Consider:

- Purchasing equipment/furniture.
- Employing someone new.
- Hiring equipment/furniture.
- Hiring services, e.g. physical help, medical, business, personnel, legal advice, mediation.

- Reallocating or relocating space, equipment, furniture.
- Reallocating or relocating tasks.

Brainstorming

Collect suggestions without judgement.

You might want to look at a smorgasbord of options. You may like to assure involvement by making this phase of problem-solving a formal *brainstorm*:

- Assemble the relevant people.
- Sometimes you might want to set a time limit: 'For the next five minutes (half an hour, or whatever) we'll just throw around ideas.' Just let ideas come until the flow runs dry.
- If the problem is complex, appoint one person to record all suggestions. If a group is involved, write up suggestions with thick, coloured Texta pens on a large sheet of butcher's paper so everyone can see the ideas going up.
- Welcome all ideas, no matter how crazy. Allow a little humour and nonsense if at all appropriate—this can release tension and generate some lateral thinking. Be bold—what seems impossible might seed good ideas.
- Accept ideas without prejudice, commitment or evaluation, to avoid stifling new possibilities or implying people should stand behind any option they come up with. During a difficult negotiation, you might choose to hold a brainstorm at a special time and define it as a process 'without prejudice' or commitment to any solutions developed during the session.

Currencies

What is cheap for me and valuable for them?

Good solution-building works on a broad front. The aim is to develop a package plan that encompasses a wide range of factors. You may offer suggestions which are easy ('low-cost') for you, and you might ask for things you know are relatively easy for the other person to give. These are the 'currencies' in which you can both trade. Currencies include services, timing, recognition and security, and become 'elegant' currencies when one person offers something low-cost to them and of high value for the other person.

If you give me something then I'll give you something.

The aim is to survey everyone's needs and sweeten the pie for yourself and for the other person with low-cost components. Often you will be able to trade concessions. In a business contract you may offer speedy delivery of something already in stock for cash on delivery instead of the monthly account payment! You may pay a lower interest rate on a loan in return for blue-chip security about your ability to repay.

The onus is on you to set up the trade-off and spell it out: 'If you give my carrier a cheque, then I'll give you those widgets by

Friday. But the deal's off if I'm not paid on delivery'; or 'I need my gutters cleaned. Have you got time this weekend? I'll make you a loaf of bread if I know you're coming.'

A note of warning: If you overdo trade-offs, the other person can feel bribed or coerced. 'You do the washing up and I'll give you money for an ice-cream' may not develop in a child the spirit of voluntary co-operation that makes a family work well.

Chunking

Sometimes you can't solve the whole problem but you can solve bits of it. When the task is huge, break the problem down into smaller, more manageable chunks. Consider what would at least help.

Break down the problem into manageable chunks.

OPTION GENERATOR

	Their needs, values, limits and priorities.		
My needs, values, limits and priorities.			

James has two children by his first marriage. He still keeps regular and devoted contact with the children. His ex-wife Elizabeth's new husband has been offered an excellent promotion in another city. It seems that the family will move and James is very upset about losing the close contact with his children. He tried chunking the problem using an option generator chart.

OPTION GENERATOR

James's needs, values, limits and priorities	Elizabeth's needs, values, limits, priorities	1. To keep the children happy	2. To support her new marriage	3. To be financially secure
1. To see the children often		Plan long school holiday visits	Go along with the planned move	Clarify agreements on child support and air fares
2. To contribute to their lives while they grow up		Take time off work when children visit		
3. To contine to be regarded as their dad		Telephone often	Telephone mainly before new husband comes home	Children to know what James provides them with

Consider a current problem, one that seems to have no simple answer. List three major needs, values, limits or priorities for both you and the other person. Consider some of the points on the Option Generator where a need of yours and a need of the other person meet. Come up with some suggestions that would help that piece of the problem. Use the Option Generator on page 133.

Best Alternatives

In designing options in a difficult situation it is thoroughly worthwhile to consider what is your best alternative if agreement cannot be made. Professional negotiators including Roger Fisher use the word BATNA (Best Alternative To a Negotiated Agreement) as shorthand for this key concept.[1] If the problem with the boss doesn't work out, your best alternative might be to look for another job. Is it worth ringing a personnel company to find out what's on their books? If you can make your alternative attractive, or at least more acceptable, you are not quite so desperate in your negotiations. Being too eager can be a disadvantage when you're bargaining. The other person can sense how badly you want something and can feel safe about not dropping the terms. Salespeople are quick to sense how keen you are to have something. Be careful when you are selling too. If you want an order too badly you may not feel secure about negotiating to a better price, or you may push too hard and lose the sale.

The other person has alternatives too. Sometimes you can present information which shows that their best alternative is not so attractive after all. If you think your boss wants to sack you and employ someone else, you could point out how long it takes to learn your job!

Consequence Confrontation

If you are dealing with someone who refuses to budge or won't listen to you, it may be important to work out what your options are. You may need to outline the consequences if they do not negotiate. Don't threaten, but present them as alternatives you otherwise will be forced to take. Save consequence confrontation as a last resort.

Consequence confrontation: Would it help or hinder?

STAGE 2: Choosing Options

The creating stage can be bypassed if needs are clearly understood. One solution may jump up straight away as the perfect resolution. However, if you have used a brainstorming session, don't move to choosing options until time is up or a good number of suggestions are on the table. In a formal session you might begin by rating each suggestion: 1. very useful; 2. lacking some elements; 3. not practicable. This helps keep participants evaluating which suggestions meet their needs or which ones do not.

Suggestions can also be evaluated according to these criteria:

• *Is it feasible?* How feasible? When can it happen?

Evaluate each option:
1. Is it feasible?
2. Is it enough?
3. Is it fair?

- *Is it enough?* Does it solve the problem? Does it satisfy everyone's needs adequately?
- *Is it fair?* What is this judgment based on? Find, if you can, an objective yardstick and collect relevant information on the options. It might be based on equality. Equivalent money, time, benefits or workloads might be considered. It might be based on precedence. Independent evaluations of market price or recent sales may be applicable. It might be based on savings such as how many hours or how much money this suggestion might save.

Your legal rights may also be relevant. What does the law say? For example, what constitutes unreasonable disturbance when sound levels are the problem? Ethics may be hard to measure, but they also have a significant place in judging what is fair.

Independent yardsticks can be very helpful when there are unrealistic expectations that need to be brought down to earth before an agreement can be reached.

STAGE 3: Action on the Chosen Options

Task performance:
By whom?
By when?
Review when?

Many a great plan fizzles for lack of follow-through. Formally or informally, set up a critical path, or at least plan the first steps.

- What are the tasks?
- Who will do what?
- By when does each task need to be done?

Plan your first steps. Discuss together what each of you will do and draft a schedule. If the solution works for you both and you have arrived at it in partnership, both sides can be reasonably trusted to carry out their part of the plan. Make sure you each understand what you have to do, and plan a specific review time.

SUMMARY

Design answers that incorporate wins for everyone.

STAGE 1: Creating Options
1. Define the problem in terms of needs.
2. Develop options together.
3. Be practical. Consider
   - Information and its flow
   - Structures and procedures
   - Objects and services

4. Brainstorming:
   - Do not debate
   - Do not justify
   - Do not censor
5. Currencies: what is cheap for me and valuable for them? And vice versa?
6. Chunking: break up the problem in smaller and more manageable portions.
7. Best alternatives: what is the best alternative if we don't agree?
8. Consequence confrontation: would it hinder or help to point out your alternatives?

STAGE 2: Choosing Options
Evaluate:

- Is it feasible?
- Is it enough?
- Is it fair?

STAGE 3: Acting on the Chosen Option

- Tasks to be performed
- By whom?
- By when?
- Review when?

NOTES
1. Roger Fisher, *Getting to Yes*, ibid (see Note 2, Chapter 1).

USEFUL READING
Edward de Bono, *Conflicts—A Better Way to Resolve Them* (London: Penguin, 1986).

CHAPTER TEN

Negotiation

Have you ever had to do any of the following:

- Ask the boss for a raise or some time off?
- Deal with too many people asking you to do things all at once?
- Buy a major appliance for the house?
- Work out who will do the household chores?
- Plan how you will live with someone else?
- Ask for permission to have a party?
- Sort out where to go on a holiday or an outing?

We negotiate throughout our lives, exchanging commitments and promises. Any time two people need to reach an agreement, they have to negotiate if the terms are not yet clear. Negotiation is what business is all about—arrangements for buying, selling or exchanging

goods and services. It is what relationships are all about, too—working or living in the same space, planning who does what and who decides what. It goes on between countries, over the exchange of products or border disputes.

Take a minute to place negotiation in the context of your life. Where do you negotiate? Which aspect of negotiating is hardest for you? When a negotiation is not going well, it's easy to see it as some sort of contest which one person will win and the other will lose. Depending on our natural tendencies and how we see our power in relation to the other person, we will go either into *fight* or *flight* mode (see Chapter 4, Appropriate Assertiveness). In fight mode the hardest thing might be controlling your temper. In flight mode perhaps the hardest thing is to stand firm and hold your ground.

The objective of a negotiation is generally not to come out on top but to reach a balanced agreement that seems fair to both parties. That's an agreement the parties will stick to.

Neither fight nor flight are likely to achieve this. What is needed is a flow of purpose, direction, power and flexibility.

PREPARATION

What practical steps help negotiations to flow?

1. Remember, conflict is opportunity.

2. Be ready at all times for discovery. A negotiation is a life-size jigsaw puzzle where you create the pieces. Look for what can work.

3. Free yourself from fixed ideas about solutions.

4. For most negotiations, the most effective preparation is to make a needs and fears map (see Chapter 8 Mapping the Conflict). Fears include anxieties, concerns and those 'I wouldn't like it if . . .'. It's particularly valuable where there's a large psychological and personality-based component in the negotiation—and there nearly always is.

What are the needs?
What are the fears?

5. Ask yourself, 'What outcome do I want?' If you want a particular outcome, what needs, values and long-term issues are you taking into consideration? Don't forget the intangibles such as recognition, security, relationship.

What outcome do you want?

6. Estimate the range of tangible results that might define this outcome. You'll have more flexibility if you set upper and lower limits. For example, 'We'd like to make $6, and below $4 it doesn't pay us to sell at all.'

Collect the facts.

7. Have the facts ready. Do your homework thoroughly, though you will rarely need to bring into conversation all the facts and possibilities you have marshalled during a good preparation. It's a bit like an exam—you don't know what area you will be tested on.

8. Work on your case.[1] Prepare concise answers to:
   (a) What do I want? What's the heart of what I intend to say?
   (b) Who am I asking? Am I approaching the right person for decision-making? Does that person have a preferred way of operating that I should take into account?
   (c) How will this person benefit? Carefully consider what their needs and interests are—and how to address them. What tactics and strategies will move them?
   (d) What can we trade? What is cheap for me to give up and valuable for them to receive? What is cheap for them to give up and valuable for me to receive? (See Currencies, Chapter 9 Designing Options)

9. Work on the other person's case, too. Try to think as they think.
   (a) How would they argue their case?
   (b) What are their options?
   (c) What are their immediate difficulties?
   (d) What are the implications for them if they say 'yes'? Are they acceptable? Can you spell out positive implications or change the plan to address the negative ones?

Make 'yes' easy to say.

   (e) What will the steps be if the other person agrees? Think the steps through for them. Can the plan be built around something that is easy for them to do? Make 'yes' easy to say by helping to lighten their follow-up tasks. Have ready information that they may need—offer to draft the letter if that's appropriate.

With some negotiations there is no time to think first. For example, the phone rings and someone springs a surprise request on you. It is often necessary and quite acceptable to explain that you need to collect more information and will get back to them. Take the time you need to prepare.

INTERACTION

First, centre yourself (see Chapter 5 Co-operative Power). Don't forget to breathe deeply first. If you're anxious, deliberately calm and deepen your breathing pattern. Next, start to build trust.

1. Remember empathy openers (see Chapter 3 Empathy) and use them where appropriate.

2. Be patient. Use active listening.

3. Use *appropriate assertiveness* to talk about your needs and the outcome you hope for without arousing defensiveness.

Listen to how it is for the other side. Tell them how it is for you.

4. Establish a win/win climate. Remember, in a truly successful negotiation everyone wins.

5. Avoid win/lose outcomes. Let's introduce a piece of negotiation language: the *zero sum game*. In a zero sum game, if I win $2 you lose $2; if a pie is a certain size and I have three-quarters of it, there is only a quarter left for you; if one person gets the promotion, the other person misses out. Zero sum games force on you the competitive win/lose mode. For sport that's fine. Competition is the challenge to accomplish something. But for personal and business relations the zero sum game is a poor tactic. Zero sum games are played on the assumption there's not enough for everyone to have what they want. People can turn sour when they don't get what they need or continually have to defend their position.

Things often look like a zero sum game, but sometimes you can introduce a new factor to change the perspective. For instance, we could see my favourite movie or yours this Saturday night— zero sum! But we *could* see one of the movies this week and the other next week and increase the size of the pie. If it seems one must lose, change the perspectives, factors or perceptions.

Can you change the perspectives?

If only one person can be promoted, the other person might broaden their perspective to consider what really are the wins for them, e.g. what did they learn from the experience? What opportunities are they still free to explore?

6. Be brief and to the point. Many a good case has been spoilt by someone being long-winded and unclear.

7. Don't be afraid to sell yourself. Have the courage of your convictions: good plans will work for both parties. People are often afraid to ask for what they really want. In truth, if other people knew what you wanted, they might at least meet you part of the way.

8. Put your case in terms of *their* needs—don't just say why *you* want something.

ASK QUESTIONS

Asking the right questions is an art (see Chapter 3 Empathy). The right question can open up and/or redirect negotiation. When should you ask a question?

Ask questions to steer the negotiation.

9. Ask questions to steer the negotiation. For example, if you feel that the negotiation is not heading in the direction you would prefer, you can change the flow with a well-placed question. For example: 'Is this plan going to get us where we want to go?'

   If you are unsure of what you want to do or say, questions can buy you time and allow you to find out more information. Rather than trying to work it out for yourself, ask: 'What else is important to you in this situation?'

• Specific 'how' or 'what' questions can cover the ground more effectively than assumptions can. When the other person expresses themselves very generally ('I want the best . . .'), ask 'What *would* be best for you?' Don't assume that you know.

• When faced with a blanket statement such as 'All my friends are allowed to . . .', try asking '*All* your friends?' Question 'every' and 'never' statements, too. In the face of 'too expensive, too much or too many', try a question that raises a comparison. For example, if you are told that air-conditioning is too expensive for the office, ask: 'Expensive in what terms?' If the terms are dollars, you could question the cost of sick days or low work output due to poor conditions.

• When faced with rigid statements such as 'We couldn't do that' or 'We always do it this way . . .', go for what *is* possible. Questions lead the mind. Frame your question to lead toward the consideration of other possibilities. Ask 'What would it take to *make* it possible?' rather than 'Why is it impossible?' When faced with can't, won't, must, mustn't, should and shouldn't, accept the difficulty and then ask some leading questions. For example:

   (a) 'I can't get the report done in time.'
   Question: 'If you were to do it in time what would you need?'
   And you might receive the reply 'Well, if I had more help, or access to more information . . .'

   (b) 'I shouldn't make a fuss about it.'
   Question: 'What would make it easier for you to approach him?'

   (c) 'I won't do what you're asking—your plan is unacceptable.'
   Question: 'What would the plan have to address in order for you to accept it?'

   (d) 'I can't come to the meeting. I'm too shy.'

Question: 'What would you need for you to feel more comfortable attending the meeting?'

- When faced with unwillingness to negotiate, or defensiveness, ask the other person what would make them *more* willing. Or interested. Or more sure about the situation.

- When faced with high emotions from the other person the temptation is to defend yourself, top them, justify your position or dig your heels in. When you feel defensive, don't defend! It's usually better to wait until you have calmed down before you respond. Instead, sidestep the emotion—sometimes it helps to move physically. Change your position to indicate a change in your mental position.

  When you feel defensive, become an active listener.

  Concentrate on active listening questions in order to learn the needs, priorities and preferences at the source of the other person's problem. Then ask a question which redirects the interaction toward a win/win outcome: 'What do you really want?', 'How can we put it right?' or 'I didn't handle that as well as I might have. Is there anything we could do now to help the situation?' If it is important to put your own case, too, use an 'I' statement after you have acknowledged the legitimacy of their unaddressed needs. Otherwise people can misinterpret the statement about your needs as a denial of theirs. If you must argue, stick to the subject under discussion. Don't drag in other issues.

10. Don't use irritants. Avoid phrases like 'Well, I'm only being fair and reasonable'. This may suggest that you are implying that they are *not* being fair and reasonable.

11. Separate the person from the problem.[3] Be hard on the problem and soft on the person. Forget about being an opponent and act as though you are partners side by side, facing the problem together. Where possible try to reinforce this physically. A board or piece of paper on which you can both make notes and from which you can read helps place you in a non-confrontational position. People can then attack what has been written down rather than each other.

   Be hard on the problem and soft on the person.

12. Include their point of view. You needn't agree with it, simply acknowledge it. For example: 'I can see your point of view. From *my* point of view it's like this . . .' Or try: 'What I like about that idea is this . . . and my concern is that . . .' Notice '*and* my concern'.

    And, not but.

    Consider the ways door close when you say 'but':
    'Come to lunch.'
    'I'd like to but I've got too much work to do.'

'Oh well, perhaps another time.'
On the other hand, doors can open with 'and':
'Come to lunch.'
'I'd love to . . . and I've got too much to do!'
'Oh, is there anything I can do to help?'

AND
not
BUT

Absorb objections by including them to make a broader picture of the whole: 'Yes, we must include your point about factory safety. How can we work that into the new plan?'

13. Set up a climate of agreement. Pay particular attention to common ground—places where your interests, priorities and concerns match each other. Talk about what you do agree about a lot. You can start spelling out the common ground at the outset. Work out together how much time you will give your meeting, then you can already say something like, 'Well, we're agreeing about the timetable, let's move on . . .'

    If stuck, go back over common ground. Each time you take a step forward in the agreement, spell it out.

    Research has shown that skilled negotiators comment over three times as much about areas of anticipated agreement and common ground than do average negotiators.[2] This technique is particularly helpful during a negotiation between parties who have little in common, and who have previously viewed each other as enemies. From time to time, restate that the objective is to reach agreement: 'Let's see how far we've gone with the agreement now.'

14. Shift unrealistic expectations. Sometimes the other person doesn't know what is reasonable or feasible. You may need to set them right about dollars, resources, time or conditions. If they think the service they want costs $50, they are going to be shocked if you're asking around $200.

    Sometimes, too, your own expectations will be unrealistic. Asking questions, taking time out to collect more facts, and staying flexible will help you to adjust your expectations. Part of your task is to close the gap between their expectations and your demands. You may need to use yardsticks of fairness (see Chapter 9 Designing Options). Talk, perhaps about hours involved or the cost of parts. It is much better to educate them *before* the bidding starts. This will save them loss of face, among other things. Before your child tells you that they want 100 children at their party, tell them you were thinking of about 20.

15. Be flexible. Negotiation is a bargaining process—you are not negotiating if all you can offer is 'Take it or leave it.' So be clear in your own mind about your range—from what you'd like, to what you would settle for. You may set a bottom line, but aim toward something above it. Without a top limit it is easy to get bidding fever and pay far too much!

    Be flexible and know your bottom line.

    Make a reasonable offer, or ask for a reasonable offer to be made, and then be prepared to negotiate further. For example, to a young teenager: 'I think 10.30 p.m. is a reasonable time for you to be home.' Your child won't agree if they were thinking more along the lines of 2 a.m.—after all, it's their first party! You'll probably end up settling on a time somewhere between 11 p.m. and midnight. Your bottom line might have been midnight—it would be great if you could pick them up early and be asleep by then.

16. What's culturally appropriate in the negotiation? The difference between the first offer and the settling price is influenced by custom. Some shops never give discounts as a matter of policy. In the market place you are able to bargain for some purchases but not for others.

    Some cultures (particularly Asian) engage in a lot of movement up and down the price scale in the bargaining process. While in other cultures (e.g. Germanic), reams of information is collected before a bid is proposed, but from then on very little negotiation of terms is possible. Other customs revolve around the amount of time spent on building a relationship between the parties before the negotiation itself is addressed. You can give offence if the customary level of formality or informality is not maintained. The giving of gifts or bribes may also need to be understood in context.

    Conflict resolving negotiators will consider carefully how far they will and won't accommodate customs. Research the cultural milieu you are negotiating within.

17. Maintain your goal, not your route. Keep your long-term purpose in sight and be flexible about how you get there. For example, Bill, an advertising account executive, devised an excellent advertising campaign and outlined it to his client, who was not, however, convinced. So Bill tried all the harder to sell his plan,

    Maintain your goal, not necessarily your route.

but was getting nowhere and, in fact, the relationship with the client was becoming very tense.

What was Bill's long-term goal? Much more than sellingthis particular campaign, he wanted a satisfied client who would maintain a relationship with the agency. He realised that he would never achieve this while the client did not trust him. Bill saw that he needed to change his approach. If a good campaign had to be sacrificed for the long-term outcome, then so be it. He began to concentrate more on the client's needs. The relationship warmed again and trust began to be re-established. In fact, within a few weeks the client quite enthusiastically accepted the original plan—with a few minor alterations to save face.

Feed off the feedback.

Bill had nearly fallen into the classic trap—'If something's not working, do more of the same'. If told firmly that something doesn't work, some people try shouting. Or if a particular line of reasoning fails to convince, they try it again and again.

18. People don't always negotiate fairly. They might talk for all the available time, be rude, ignore you, throw in red herrings or come up with unreasonable demands. See the diagram for some conflict resolving counter-tactics:

19. Take notes. Many negotiations require a number of meetings. Some negotiations may extend over years so accurate note taking becomes crucial. Always take your own notes even if someone else is formally writing up the minutes. There is enormous potential to distort or misinterpret a conversation while minute taking. Use your notes to check the accuracy of the minutes. Use your notes to reopen negotiations just where you left them. Use them to prepare for similar negotiations.

20. Know when to stop:
    (a) If emotions run too high, call a break.
    (b) If the situation reaches an impasse, leave it alone for a day or so.
    (c) If someone uses an unfair tactic that throws you offbalance, give yourself time out. Go to the bathroom or make a cup of coffee. Centre yourself before responding.
    (d) Deflect to another topic if an issue becomes too hot.
    (e) If you think information is being withheld, take a break and talk to people separately.
    (f) Sometimes a negotiation just won't work, even though you have tried everything. Break off in a way that makes it possible to return to the negotiation on some other occasion.

CONFLICT RESOLVING COUNTER-TACTICS

Ask a question

Let some hostile remarks pass

Reframe hostile remarks

Write what is being said

Ask them to positively rephrase

Uncover their tactic by telling them that you are aware of it

Speak calmly

Agree to discuss later

Use humour

Change tack

Call time-out

Show me why that's fair

'Please tell me what you heard me say.'

Can it be dealt with privately?

CLOSING

Assessing the agreement. These questions may help you decide if an agreement will work well:

- Have both parties really chosen this contract?
- Will the agreement resolve or at least manage the problem?
- Can both parties really fulfil their promises?
- Is the agreement specific enough about when, where, how, who and how much?
- Is it balanced—do both sides share the responsibility for making it work?
- Is a follow-up or review time built into the plan?

Confirm your agreement. In informal negotiations, summarise what has been agreed to. It's always worth going over an agreement in case the other person has understood it differently to you. Jot down the terms. It's amazing how bad memories can be about agreements six months down the track!

Clear contracts prevent future conflicts.

In business it usually pays to document the agreement and provide both parties with a copy. Documentation can take the form of a memo, an invoice, an exchange of letters or a formal contract. In the home, it is surprisingly valuable to post on the refrigerator significant agreements about such matters as the division of chores. The purpose of a clear contract is to prevent future conflict.

When you reach an agreement, stop, acknowledge—and celebrate!

SUMMARY

Preparation
1. What are the needs? What are the fears? What outcome do you want?
2. Collect the facts.
3. Work on the other person's case as well as your own.
4. Make 'yes' easy to say.

Interaction
1. Listen to how it is for the other side. Tell them how it is for you.
2. In a truly successful negotiation, everyone wins.
3. Avoid win/lose outcomes. If it seems that one person must lose, can you change the perspective?
4. There is no harm in asking. Be brief and to the point. Ask questions to steer the negotiation.
5. Separate the person from the problem. Be hard on the problem and soft on the person.

6. Include objections. Use *and* not *but.* Set up a climate of agreement.
7. Be flexible. Know your bottom line. Maintain your goal, but not necessarily your route. Change unrealistic expectations. What is culturally appropriate for the negotiation?
8. Feed off the feedback. If something's not working, try a different approach.

The Close
Clear contracts prevent future conflicts.

NOTES
1. See Milo Frank, *How to Get Your Point Across in 30 Seconds or Less* (UK: Corgi, 1987).
2. Neil Rackman and John Carlisle, *The Effective Negotiator—Part 2. Planning for Negotiations* (*Journal of European Industrial Trainers* 2, 7, 1978).
3. Roger Fisher and William Ury, *Getting to Yes,* ibid.

USEFUL READING
Bill Scott, *The Skills of Negotiating* (UK: Management Skills Library, 1981).
Roger Fisher and Scott Brown, *Getting Together* (Boston: Houghton/Mifflin, 1988).

CHAPTER ELEVEN

Mediation

Skilful mediation can become part of everyday life. With mediation techniques you can turn other people's fights into fair play. It is an opportunity to put into practice the conflict resolution skills outlined in this book.

Are there conflicts around you in need of outside assistance? If so, do they involve any of the following?

- Divorce, particularly where children are involved?
- Racial and sexual discrimination or harrassment?
- Unions and management?
- Two conflicting organisations?
- Superiors and subordinates in a work setting?
- Peers or team members?
- Teachers, principal, students or parents?
- Environmental issues?
- Family members?
- Friends?
- Neighbours?

Mediation means coming between hostile parties and helping them move toward a resolution. A mediator aims for an objective and neutral stance. The role may be formally appointed or informally assumed.

The mediator helps both parties achieve what they need.

A mediator is an independent party to a problem. Generally they are not directly involved except through their attempts to turn the opponents into partners. A mediator makes sure that each party not only expresses their own side, but listens to the other side, and then moves both sides on to find solutions that satisfy them all.

A wide variety of conflict resolution procedures are available when disputants need help. Mediation is the method we will emphasise in this chapter, but it's important to know that alternatives exist which offer both more and less control over the process and outcome. The range starts from an outside ruling by a court judge and progresses to complete self-direction.

CONFLICT RESOLUTION PROCEDURES

Common Australian Usage

With third party

- Ruling: Third party hears the case. Makes a binding decision. A common management and child-rearing practice. *Court system and arbitration.*

- Recommendation: Third party gathers facts and arguments. Makes a recommendation with substantial weight. Non-binding, invites compromise. *Conciliation.*

- Go-between: Third party sees each disputant separately. Carries options and offers backwards and forwards between them. Sometimes makes suggestions. Has great power to selectively inform. *Shuttle diplomacy, conciliation.*

Control

- Process controller: Third party has tight control over process but not contents. Forgoes power to decide or recommend. Assists parties to isolate issues and options, and to reach a settlement by consensus that jointly satisfies their needs. *Mediation.*

- Process provider: Third party brings participants together, usually providing facilities. Steers parties in the use of a particular set of dispute resolution procedures. *Facilitation, conciliation.*

- Adviser on content: One participant consults an expert in the particular field, e.g. a property adviser or a stockbroker. Adviser provides data on effective practices. *Expert appraisal.*

- Adviser on process: One participant consults an expert in conflict resolution and mediation to receive assistance in presenting their own case well. *Conflict counselling.*

With participant

- Self-direction: Parties work directly with each other toward exchanging promises and commitments in order to resolve their difficulties. *Negotiation.*

FORMAL AND INFORMAL MEDIATION

Formal structures now operating in our society offer mediation (where the decision-making rests with the disputants) as an alternative to legal and other traditional methods of dealing with disputes. Mediation services are widely offered in the United States and Canada, and are expanding in other countries, too.[1] Community Justice Centres, Unifam's Family Mediation Centres and Neighbourhood Mediation Centres in Australia offer this kind of service for local, personal disputes between neighbours, family members, landlords and tenants, and other individuals whose problems are often unresponsive to conventional legal remedies. Organisations such as the Australian Commercial Disputes Centre offer mediation to industry as a faster, more equitable and definitely cheaper alternative to traditional courtroom methods. A growing number of community care organisations, counselling centres and private legal practices are offering mediation as part of their services. Many of these professional organisations will offer a mediating team of two or more chosen for their expertise in the problem area or for their compatibility with the clients. The Australian Government has also introduced schemes whereby 'grievance officers' are appointed and trained as mediators to deal with inequality, harassment and other conflicts within government departments. The role of Equal Employment Opportunity and Affirmative Action officers is most frequently one of mediation, too.

Mediation can be a very simple process. Children as young as seven years of age are being taught about it in schools. Once taught teenagers can use it very powerfully to resolve problems with peers. Many schools have found a significant boost in morale and a corresponding drop in disciplinary problems by introducing a mediation program. An interested teacher or counsellor usually acts as co-ordinator.[2]

Many people are drawn to conflict resolution skills because they want to help others. As people of good will, they are aware that unresolved conflict is destructive and they want to improve the situation. You may find yourself drawn into conflict situations in the following ways:

Resist advising. Offer options not directions.

1. Conflict counselling. How many times have friends or colleagues come to you when they are having a problem with someone else? These are opportunities to take on the role of conflict counsellor and help them deal constructively with their situation by using a win/win approach. Resist the temptation to tell them what you think they should do. Any suggestions should be offered as options, not directions. Leave them free to do something quite

different if they wish. Don't become caught up in agreeing how awful the situation is and how right they are. Don't make their enemies your enemies. Even if you *do* think they are right, your overt agreement gives them 'permission' to stay stuck. Generally you can move them further by helping them to look at the other side and see how they can change the situation.

2. Informal mediation. When are you likely to mediate? First, you need to recognise that the people in conflict are not coping well alone and need outside help. Then you need to be motivated and able to assist at the time they *need* help. It's best if you don't have a vested interest other than the desire to reach a successful outcome for both parties.

   In informal mediation you will want the conflict to be resolved speedily if it presents *you* with problems, in your close working or living relationships. As an informal mediator you may sometimes be invited by both parties to participate; sometimes *you* might make the offer; sometimes you may work directly with only one party at a time; and sometimes the situation may be so informal that you are mediating without the other parties even noticing!

MAGGIE'S STORY

I was in line to buy a ticket at the railway station and it was almost time for my train to arrive. The old man in front of me kept asking for a refund on a ticket he couldn't use but the clerk kept telling him that he would actually have to present the ticket. The old man would nod and say 'yes'—and continue asking for the refund. It became apparent that the old man was very deaf. The clerk was becoming quite irate and kept repeating, 'Bring in your ticket', more and more loudly. Yet the old man kept nodding and wouldn't leave. The line grew longer and time was ticking away.

Although I was ready to scream, I took a deep breath, centred myself and looked for the win/win. I asked the clerk, 'Would it help if you wrote it down for the old man?'

'No,' he said, 'he wouldn't understand.'

'Might there be someone he could take it away and show it to?' I asked, floating another option. The clerk grunted, wrote some instructions down and the old man went away. As I purchased my ticket, I asked the clerk, 'What's it like for you when something like that happens?' The clerk briefly expressed his frustration, relaxed a bit, and then said, 'Gee, it must be hard for that old man. I wonder how he gets through his day?'

Maggie had been supportive of both people. Writing the instructions down was the best thing for both the old man and the ticket clerk. It also got the line moving again so that Maggie could be served, too.

There will be times when emotions are highly charged and your own problem-solving reaches an impasse. At these times bringing in a mediator will be your most constructive approach to the conflict. Life is made up of ever-turning circles—we might be a mediator one day and need one the next. From all these experiences and interchanges we learn and grow. Mediation is a service we can offer each other if we trust the process.

SETTING IT UP

Turn opponents into problem-solving partners.

You don't have to be invited to mediate. Instead you could introduce the possibility of an informal mediation roughly this way: 'I know you two are in conflict. Sometimes it's easier to work these things out better with someone there to help steer the ship. I'd like to help you move toward something that works for both of you. My contribution would be to get together with you and help this happen. I'd support both of you and not take sides. I won't come up with answers or judgments and I'll do my best to remain objective.'

One party can also apply these concepts to encourage another party to participate in a mediation. It is quite common for only one party to actively seek mediation—the other party or parties need only to agree to try it. When you have that agreement, decide upon a time and a place. Your aim will be to turn opponents into problem-solving partners.

MEDIATION MADE SIMPLE

1. Make your agreements:

As mediator you will need to introduce and explain your role. Here are some of the points you should make:
- We're here to solve a problem.
- No blaming.
- No excuses.
- No interrupting.
- Tell the truth.

2. Listen to everyone:
- Each person tells what has happened to them, while the others listen.
- Each person repeats what is said, to make sure they understood.
- Each person then tells how *they* feel.

3. Resolve the conflict
- Each person explains what they need if they are to reach agreement.
- The mediator helps both sides to decide on a fair agreement.
- The agreement can be written down and signed by each person.

A good start to learning to mediate is a thorough grounding in the general conflict resolution skills outlined in this book. How do they apply in the context of mediation?

Demonstrate a better way to manage differences.

CONFLICT RESOLUTION SKILLS

You will probably be proving the effectiveness of conflict resolution skills in your own life, so as mediator you can demonstrate to the parties a better way to manage their differences. The mediation process then becomes a learning and developing experience for the participants. What they learn from this mediation they can put to good use in future conflict situations.

For effective interaction, the mediator uses all the skills of conflict resolution, as follows:

1. *The win/win approach*—set the scene so both parties tackle the problem together.

2. *The creative response*—you may need to lead the protagonists out of despair and into a search for opportunity. The conflict may conceal unexplored possibilities. Notice negative statements and reframe them to form positive ones. For example, 'It could be very helpful that this argument has come up between you. It's a splendid opportunity to rethink directions', or 'I can see that this problem will allow you both to become closer.'

3. *You need empathy.* Being neutral means you work for the best results for both parties. Let each party know that you care about them. Be aware of a lack of empathy in others. Encourage active listening on both sides by example.

4. *Operate with appropriate assertiveness.* Encourage the same in all parties to the conflict. Use and encourage 'I' statements. If you feel uncomfortable with what is being said, try something like, 'I'm feeling uncomfortable about that last statement' or 'I might not have explained the process well enough. I think it would work better if . . .'

5. *Move the participants toward the co-operative use of power.* Your role as mediator is very powerful and you can assist particularly if one party has been coercing the other party or parties. You'll need:
(a) Active neutrality, balancing the power of both sides to give each party equal time to talk and to ask questions to expose information which may be important.
(b) Personal power. Start by being centred—it helps you to be more sure that you will do next whatever is most appropriate. You can help participants with their personal power by encouraging them to take responsibility and choose positive action. Ask questions such as 'What can *you* do?' or 'What's one thing that would make a difference?'

6. *Managing emotions* is a valuable mediation skill. It's up to you to keep calm. Steer the participants so that they neither deny emotions nor indulge them. Allow feelings to be expressed without blaming the other party. Openly acknowledge the significant emotions of a participant: 'You're finding this very upsetting.'

7. *A mediator obviously has a willingness to resolve.* To create this in the conflicting parties, however, can be a major challenge.

8. *Lead the exploration of needs and fears of all involved by mapping the conflict.* Direct the process (but not the content) and act as a recorder.

9. *Initiate a designing options phase.* If you enrich your own life with well-designed options, you'll already have skills to help the parties create more choices for themselves. Identify any new information arising in the session that could unfold new options. Ask for suggestions. Possibly brainstorm. Don't weigh up suggestions too early in the piece.

A desert shiek died, bequeathing his nineteen camels to his three sons, leaving his first son half his camels, his second son a quarter of his camels, and his third son a fifth of his camels. As it isn't economical to carve up camels, the three sons invited a mediator, who arrived on his *camel. The mediator assessed the situation and lent this camel to the estate. There were now twenty camels. The first son received his half (ten camels),* the second son his quarter (five camels), and the third son his fifth (four camels). This added up to the nineteen camels left in the estate, leaving the mediator with the camel he came with. He mounted it and rode away.

    Had you been the mediator, would you have felt that justice was done? Or would you have asked awkward questions like: What about the sheik's daughters . . .?

---

10. *Effective negotiation skills* are of great value in mediation. Your orientation and the one you encourage the participants to use is hard on the problem and soft on the person. Shift 'buts' to 'ands'. Include objections when you are building up a complete picture.

STEPS IN MEDIATION

At the Beginning

1. Attention to seating is important. It is better not to have opponents sitting opposite each other.

2. Have a big board or a sheet of paper and pens for mapping or recording significant aspects of the problem.

3. Decide upon timing. How long will the meeting last? Seek a commitment for everyone to stay to the end of this time. If it seems unlikely that you will finish in one session you may plan future sessions at the beginning of this initial meeting or at the end.

4. Clarify the role of the mediator. Emphasise that you will not be judging the situation. Your task is to assist with procedures, the disputants are in charge of content.

You *steer the* process. They are *in charge of the* content.

5. To facilitate openness you may offer to respect confidentiality. Professional mediators would normally do so. The participants may or may not want to make a similar agreement.

6. Make sure procedures and agreements are clear from the outset and that everyone agrees to them. Check if anyone wants to add something more. Agreements can be added to or re-negotiated at any time if one party is not happy.

7. One or both parties may have come to the mediation unwillingly. You need to check that they are at least prepared to give the process a go. Their commitment to it will improve if they can acknowledge, now or by the end of the session, that the process could or has been helpful. Reassure them that their hesitancy is normal.

Have them speak from their own perspective.

8. Make an agreement with all parties that they will use 'I' statements. Ask them to begin statements with 'From my experience . . .', 'As I see it . . .', or 'It's my opinion that . . .' so that all statements are seen in a personal context or perspective, and are not presented as indisputable facts or generalisations. Participants should avoid blaming or putting interpretations onto the behaviour of the other party. For example: 'You keep your music turned up just to annoy me' should be said this way instead, 'When your music is loud I find it hard to study and I become really annoyed.' Ask the participants to talk about the problem they are having.

9. Find the focus. It is usually helpful at the start of a mediation to identify the general areas in which the parties want to reach agreement. There are two possible focus points for a mediation session:
   (a) Future—This is the most usual focus. The past is regarded as water under the bridge and the discussion is moved rapidly away from old anger and pain to 'What do we do now?' By concentrating on a future focus, most people who have absorbed conflict resolution skills well can mediate well. In most workplace circumstances future focus mediations are the most appropriate and the most effective. Many professional mediation agencies will only lead future focus mediations.
   (b) Past—Sometimes conflicts from the past need to be resolved. Occasionally, both parties need to resolve their pent-up feelings toward each other, and the only way for them to deal with the present disagreement is to re-examine old issues. Past hurts and significant misunderstandings of motives can block present relationships. 'Clearings' are most

CAROL'S STORY

Recently I watched helplessly as two of my closest friends ended their relationship. They mixed in the same social and business circles and unfortunately when they attended the same functions they became angry with one another very easily. It was very uncomfortable for those around them as well as for themselves. In the end it became such a problem that one of them would not attend a function if they knew that the other had been invited. Finally, I couldn't stand it any more, so I offered to mediate for them. They said they'd give it a try.

A week later we met on neutral territory (the beach!), made agreements about how we would operate together, and set a time limit. The purpose of the mediation was to reach an agreement for handling social situations.

I then allowed some time for each to speak out, constantly checking that the other listened without become defensive. After a while, they both softened a little toward each other as they acknowledged the good times they had had, along with the present difficulties. They then agreed that when they met socially they would immediately acknowledge each other with a special greeting in recognition of their past closeness and because each had recently annoyed the other by not greeting them at all.

They also agreed that after greeting each other they would keep at a friendly distance for a while. There was still a lot of hurt and anger between them and more time was needed for it to heal before a more comfortable friendship could develop. It wasn't part of my brief that day to sort out the difficulties that had led them to part. We had come together to look at what they would do now. The focus was on the future. It was enough that each now felt comfortable at the same functions—neither would have to miss out because the other was planning to attend.

commonly needed in ongoing intimate relationships. It takes skilled counselling and is usually best left to a professional therapist.

10. Make sure that the parties participate equally. It's not important who goes first, as long as it's clear that both will have a chance to express their point of view. At the beginning and throughout the process, keep checking that both parties are having a fair say and really listening to each other.

During the Process

Keep the process moving forward. The destination is win/win. Remember to create a safe atmosphere where each party can lower their defences, open up and become willing to shift, give, share, examine, reconsider and jointly resolve the problem. Once it has been set up the process will sometimes flow without you needing to intervene much at all. At other times you will need to call on the 'tool kit' available to the mediator:

1. *Mapping* is an excellent tool, since the participants then can all

Map the conflict wherever possible.

see each other's needs and concerns about the issue, and find things that change the picture or open up possibilities.

2. *Summarising* key points is useful for everyone. Restate core messages using a format that opens options. For example, 'You're not happy with things as they are and you would like to find some ways to improve the situation.' To stop a monologue, summarise the point, confirm you understand it correctly and ask a question that may direct the conversation forward.

At times it may be helpful when one person has spoken, to encourage the other(s) to summarise what has been accurately said before responding. This technique is particularly helpful if one person significantly changes their attitude or makes a concession. People frequently do not absorb information which would require them to change their perception of the other person or of the situation. When emotions run high it is very useful to ask each person to 'mirror' what the other has said before they explain how they feel themselves.[3]

Point out where they agree.

3. *Define the common ground* where both parties agree or have similar needs. For example, 'You both want what's best for the children.'

4. *Offer suggestions only if you can make it sound like an option and not a direction.* For example, 'I heard of a situation in which a couple solved a similar problem about finances by having a joint account to which they contributed equally, as well as their own separate accounts. Would that be relevant here?'

5. *Allow silences.* They give everyone time to think and integrate ideas.

6. *Offer breaks.* When emotions run high it is good to call a cooling-off period of perhaps ten or fifteen minutes so that each person can go for a walk. Whatever the emotional climate, if you've been meeting for more than an hour and a half then you will all really appreciate a little time out from the process.

7. *Future orientation.* Ask each party to create their vision of the future with the outcome they want. Ask 'How would you like it to be?' or 'What would it look like if it was all working well?' For future-focused mediations the past is relevant insofar as it provides necessary information for decision-making in the current context. Emphasising a future orientation can stop short any mudslinging, accusations and rearoused resentment.

8. *Positive orientation.* If someone is harping about the things they *don't* want, ask them to tell you what they *do* want.

9. *Action orientation.* Questions which might make the parties want to take action can include 'What can *you* do to make the outcome as you want it?' or 'Where do we go from here?'

You might set homework tasks. One clever mediator who worked with a disfunctional family, including a withdrawn teenage girl, asked the girl to log the day, time and topic of each of her parents' arguments. The parents had their own tasks but they knew that they were being observed by their daughter. The task encouraged the girl to move out of her isolation and participate in the solution. By carrying out the task she indicated that she was prepared to take part in the therapy.

A skilled mediator may develop a repertoire of effective activities to suggest when dealing with commonly observed problems.

10. Sometimes you may want to use a question to reframe a conflict creating concept (see Chapter 10 Negotiation).

CONFLICT ANTIDOTES

Conflict Creators	Reframing Questions
You fool! (and other insults)	What do you need? How can it be fixed?
I'm right. You (or they) are wrong.	How would you say your point of view differs from theirs?
I won't . . .	What would make you willing?
It's a failure.	How could it work? What would make it better?
He (she) is hopeless!	What are they doing that's OK?
I (they) should/ought/must/ have to . . .	Would you (they) *choose* to take up that option?
Too many/much/little/few . . .	Compared to what?
They always . . .	Are there any circumstances in which they don't?
I don't want . . .	What do you want to happen?
I can't . . .	You can't? Or you just can't see a way to? What happens if you do?
He (she) would never . . .	How can we find ways for it to happen?
It's impossible.	But if it *were* possible, what would it take?

11. *Normalise experiences* that the person regards as extraordinary or outrageous. For example, the participant might accuse, 'She wouldn't even speak to me!' and you can explain, 'It is not uncommon in this type of argument to need a cooling-off period in which the parties *don't* speak to each other.' Or if someone storms out of the mediation because the other party was too blunt, then say something like, 'We all have strong reactions sometimes. Can we come back and try again?'

Looking from the opposite point of view breaks down rigid thinking.

12. *Help create new perspectives.* For example: to an ex-husband who is not doing much for his children, 'What if you went to court and custody of your children was awarded to you? What would life be like for you?' Ask the protagonists to picture a scenario that puts them in the other person's shoes, or in a 'What if . . .' situation. Pose questions about what it would be like, invite them to reassess rigid or limited attitudes. You might ask a 'self-righteous' non-smoker to consider how they would feel if they were addicted to cigarettes.

Respect individual differences.

13. *Clarify and validate differences* in values, personal styles and points of view. For example, 'To you, Jane, dress codes are very important, but John needs to express his individuality with his clothes', 'It's quite understandable that after dinner Mary's first priority is to do the dishes while yours, Peter, is to relax' or 'You're naturally reserved, Alison, and Sarah likes to be upfront. You'll probably both have to stretch your styles a bit so that you can meet halfway.'

Balance dissatisfaction between parties who want to punish each other.

14. *Balancing dissatisfaction.* Sometimes (as in a difficult divorce) by the time a mediator is called, emotions are running very high and animosity is rampant. Neither party wants the other to win. In fact, each wants the other party to be punished. The most the mediator can hope for is to end up with both parties equally *dissatisfied* with the settlement. As long as the other side is not doing too well either, the trade-offs each is required to make will be acceptable. Such outcomes may not provide much fulfilment for the mediator, but as a last resort they may settle the problem and give both parties a chance to get on with their lives.

At the End

You will need to bring the session to an end with at least some agreements made by the parties. You may decide to meet again. You may set them or remind them of tasks that they are prepared to go away and try.

1. Summarise and, where possible, write down agreements for each

party. People find these documents very important. It gives them something concrete to take away and serves as future reference.

2. You might ask them to set up a yardstick to measure effective change. It may include measurement of how many disagreements have occurred during one week; how much time has been needed to complete a job; the amount of time spent communicating with each other in a week; the number of family outings in a month; or the frequency of recurrence of a mediated problem (e.g. noise disturbance).

   Ask them to make a specific time to review how they are progressing, what is working and what needs some adjustment. Ask them to describe how they will correct a problem if things don't work as expected.

3. After the mediation is over, acknowledge the participation and contribution of each party.

4. Celebrate! Will participants exchange a handshake, share a meal or a hug? Do you, the mediator, want to join in too?

Mediators need to be wary of the enticements of playing the role of rescuer, while remembering that there are genuine victims in need of protection from danger, exploitation and injustice. Training helps you steer between these dangers.

Mediation is a valuable resource for any community. Everyone benefits by education and information about mediation. Mediation is not a mysterious process that can only be offered by elitist professionals. The process is a natural extension of good conflict resolution skills. Mediation turns opponents into problem-solving partners.

SUMMARY

A mediator helps both parties achieve what they need. The process demonstrates how conflict resolution skills provide a better way to manage differences.

Steps in Mediation

In the beginning: Arrange seating, recording of the meeting and timing. Clarify your role: you steer the process, the disputants are in charge of the content. Discuss commitments, 'I' statements, focus and equal participation.

During the process: Use mapping, summarising and silences. Define common ground. Make suggestions as options and not as directions. Allow silences and breaks. Maintain future, positive and action orientations. Use questions to reframe conflict-creating concepts. Normalise experiences. Create new perspectives by asking participants to speak from opposite points of view to their own. Validate differences. Balance dissatisfactions when the parties only want to punish each other.

At the end: Make some agreements. Write them down. How can they measure effective change? Ask them to make time to review progress. Acknowledge participation and celebrate—you've earned it!

Mediation turns opponents into problem-solving partners.

NOTES

1. For more information contact:
   The Conflict Resolution Network
   PO Box 1016
   Chatswood NSW 2057
   Australia
   (Tel): (02) 419 8500

2. See above.

3. Christopher Hills, *Creative Conflict* (California: University of the Trees Press, 1980).

CHAPTER TWELVE

Broadening Perspectives

The win/win approach takes a broader approach than the limited, although frequently used, win/lose. Many conflicts can be resolved by taking the broader perspective of 'me-and-you' instead of 'me-or-you'. But sometimes even this wider view is not sufficient to solve a problem effectively—we need the whole picture.

To build up complete pictures an understanding of General Systems Theory is useful:

> 'General Systems Theory . . . sees the world as an interconnected hierarchy of matter and energy. According to this view, nothing can be understood on its own; everything is part of a system (a system being defined in its most general sense as a set of units which are related to each other and interact). Systems may be abstract, as in mathematical systems and metaphysical systems, or concrete, as in a telephone system or transport system.
>
> One branch of General Systems Theory deals particularly with living systems . . . All living systems are composed of sub-systems which take in, process, and put out matter, energy or information or a combination of these.'[1]

Think of the planet as a giant clock with millions of big and little interacting cogs and you will have a passable image of what systems theory is all about. It forms a theoretical foundation for many modern management practices and for futurist warnings and advice.

The skill of Broadening Perspectives lies in seeing the fundamental interconnectedness of all things, and in taking into account a wider system than the one immediately apparent when only looking at individual needs. If we recognise that we are working within a network of open, living, interacting systems, what perspectives can we then look for to handle conflict?

We need a holistic .view. To consider only one cog (a single individual or a group) is to take too narrow a view of the social

system. The effectiveness of mapping often lies in considering the needs of other groups as well as those of the main protagonists.

The union leader whose only aim is to put more money in the pockets of his members has missed some highly relevant factors. He must take a broader view and interact within wider ranging social systems, taking into account the effect of strikes on the wider community, the need to marshal support for his members' claim, the economic viability of the employer, as well as run-on effect on inflation.

In rejecting a union claim, an employer intent only on maximising profits may be failing to consider prevailing economic conditions, awards granted to other unions and perhaps the incentive value of attractive wages.

We need to correct exploitative practices. An individual or group which expands by abusing other sub-systems can eventually cause the larger system to work inefficiently, or even to break down. An example of this short-sighted view is the way mankind has handled (or mishandled) the environment without considering resultant problems of widespread pollution, increasing greenhouse effects and ozone layer damage. Many industrial and consumer practices use up non-renewable resources without any thought to the long-term effects. If we take broader perspective and a more far-sighted view, then our industry, our personal lifestyles, our disposal of waste must be ecologically sound.

There is the need for synergy (working together) between

closely interconnecting systems so that no one part is struggling against the other. In any organisation unresolved internal conflict caused by the misalignment of individual, departmental or organisational needs to the whole, can cause inefficiency and sometimes the complete breakdown of the organisational structure. The skills needed to create the synergy are those offered in this book. And, as well, aligned goal-setting at all levels is required.

A time perspective needs to be included. Are we supporting or resisting inevitable forces for change and growth? There is a pressure on living systems to evolve toward greater internal order, or to risk degeneration and extinction. Few systems can maintain an undisturbed status quo for long. In the industrial system the evolution takes place in technology. One hundred years ago, no-one flew in aeroplanes, watched pictures on television, or walked on the moon. Evolution takes place in a society within the collective beliefs and ethical standards of that social order. One hundred years ago, many people did not see the necessity of giving women the vote, and a woman's true place was thought to be in the home. Slavery was still widely accepted. Less than thirty years ago Aboriginal people were still having their children forcibly taken from them as a result of the misdirected benefactory zeal of the white community.

Where are we heading in the evolution of ideas? Many practices rest on an outdated world view in desperate need of reform. In many countries, women are still fighting for equal pay. How long before every individual understands that they have a role in the protection of the environment? How long before we re-think the so-called democratic practice which pits a government against a single or combined party opposition, and which not only limits the effectiveness of a high number of our elected representatives, but condones mud-slinging and point-scoring as a legitimate way to run the country? When will the press be held responsible for the situations they exacerbate by sensationalised reporting? When will the media see themselves as leaders in the solution of community conflict?

Some of our beliefs owe their origin to the collective thinking of past eras. Other beliefs belong to the future; these beliefs are not yet widespread enough to form part of the collective beliefs of our society. In the nineteenth century, John Stuart Mill wrote that 'every age held opinions that subsequent generations found not only false but absurd'.[2] The perspective to maintain is one in which we can accept the inevitability of flux and change.

Remember that points of view or priorities that cannot be changed right now are unlikely to remain the same forever: transforming forces are at work below the surface. But people still fight over beliefs as if they were eternal facts. Consider the public outcry against draft dodgers in the 1960s. Many people still feel sure that human nature is rooted in a win/lose approach so that war is a natural outcome. Their belief is that 'it's a dog-eat-dog world'. Perhaps one day when win/win is seen as the triumph of commonsense, a win/lose philosophy of life will appear absurd and barbaric. In a nuclear age war is no longer a win/lose strategy: any war is likely to be lose/lose.

As we approach the twenty-first century, win/win alternatives look much more tempting, particularly in international politics or in the global environment. We need to take an approach where everyone can win.

We need to include a global perspective which sees the individual, society and the planet as one whole system where each part affects the whole. We need a concept of internationalism. This need not imply any loss of national identity at the same time. Golda Meir, a former Prime Minister of Israel, said 'Internationalism does not mean the end of individual nations. Orchestras don't mean the end of violins.'[3]

Gwynne Dyer, author and narrator of the television series, *War*, said:

> 'Some generation of mankind was eventually bound to face the task of abolishing war, because civilisation was bound to endow us sooner or later with the power to destroy ourselves. We happen to be that generation, though we did not ask for the honour and do not feel ready for it. There is nobody wiser who will take the responsibility and solve this problem for us. We have to do it ourselves.'

We should all turn our attention to areas of international relations that traditionally were left in the hands of experts—but experts sometimes see only their own point of view. It's easy to dismiss nuclear disarmament activists as gullible 'peaceniks' and equally easy to dismiss as 'warmongers' those who have the security of the nation in their hands.

This kind of stereotyping and simplistic thinking won't solve a problem of such magnitude. One cannot dismiss a country's legitimate security needs, but plainly a military response forms only a small part of that security. A deeper level of security is mutually assured if a network of valued relationships can be formed, creating an atmosphere in which conflicts are resolved by dealing with everybody's needs.

If this can be achieved, the armed forces and the peacebuilders become partners not opponents. A peaceful and relationship-building international approach is as much a national defence strategy as war, weapons or confrontation.

The Bilateral Peace Treaties Proposal of the United Nations Association of Australia offers strong foundations for international security. It aims to establish a network of one-to-one relationships in international affairs. It asks that each state offers to other member-states of the United Nations a Bilateral Peace Treaty containing two proposals:

1. We will settle all disputes between us by negotiation or other peaceful means.
2. We will never be the first to resort to force, violence or war on each other or another.

Signing and celebrating Bilateral Peace Treaties[4] which contain such agreements are invaluable peacebuilding exercises.

The cynic says that it is human nature to solve our problems violently. True. But human nature only makes war possible—it does

not make war inevitable. Broad perspectives are required to deal effectively with all the components that make up world peace. Each community member has a part to play. International security rests on a foundation of peaceful and conflict-resolving community relations. In other words, intranational peace lies at the core of international peace. Ordinary people solving problems effectively build the conflict-resolving community. Conflict-resolving communities are the building blocks of a peaceful world.

It takes strength to acknowledge other points of view and other perspectives without succumbing to them. A belief in truth and justice gives us that strength. Beliefs resting on falsehood or greed can be corrected if we are willing to take the broader view. Broadening our perspective is like climbing higher up a mountain to see the further horizons. Only from these higher perspectives can we find meaning in distressing events and seemingly unconnected circumstances. Only from these higher perspectives can we begin to envisage a world that works for everyone. Only from these higher perspectives can we learn to behave as a global community and to think like a planet.

NOTES

1. Peter Russel, *The Awakening Earth* (London: Ark Paperbacks, 1982, pp 13–17).
2. Marilyn Ferguson, *The Aquarian Conspiracy* (Los Angeles: J. P. Tancher Inc., 1980, pp 197).
3. Benjamin B. Ferencz and Ken Keyes Jr, *Planethood* (Coos Bay: Vision Books, p. 44).
4. For a free booklet on the Bilateral Peace Treaties Proposal (or the other activities of The Network) contact:
   The Conflict Resolution Network
   PO Box 1016
   CHATSWOOD NSW 2057 AUSTRALIA
   (02) 419 8500.

CONFLICT CHECKLIST

It's Time To Take Action
Walk a Problem Through These Questions

1. WIN/WIN

What is my real need here? ....

....

What is theirs? ....

....

Do I want it to work for both of us? ....

2. CREATIVE RESPONSE

What opportunities can this situation bring? ....

....

Rather than 'how it's supposed to be', can I see possibilities in 'what is'? ....

....

3. EMPATHY

What is it like to be in their shoes? ....

....

What are they trying to say? ....

....

Have I really heard them? ....

....

Do they know I'm listening? ....

....

4. APPROPRIATE ASSERTIVENESS

What do I want to change? ....

....

How will I tell them this without blaming or attacking? ....

....

Is this a statement about how I feel, rather than what is right or wrong? ....

....

(Be soft on the people, hard on the problem.)

5. CO-OPERATIVE POWER

Am I using power inappropriately? ....

Are they? ....

Instead of opposing each other, can we co-operate? ....

....

6. MANAGING EMOTIONS

What am I feeling? ....

....

Am I blaming them for my feelings? ....

....

Will telling them how I feel help the situation? ....

....

What do I want to change? ....

....

Have I removed the desire to punish from my response? ....

What can I do to handle my feelings? *(e.g. write it down, talk to a friend, punch a mattress.)*

....

7.   *WILLINGNESS TO RESOLVE*

Do I want to resolve the conflict? . . . .

Is resentment being caused by

* something in my past that still hurts? . . . .
* something I haven't admitted to needing? . . . .
* something I dislike in them, because I won't accept it in myself? . . . .

. . . .

8.   *MAPPING THE CONFLICT*

What's the issue, problem or conflict?
Who are the important parties in this conflict?
Write down each person's needs. *(i.e. What interests underly the problem? What are the payoffs from suggested solutions?)*
Write down each person's anxieties or fears. *(i.e. What worries, anxieties, concerns are influencing behaviour?)*

Does this map show areas we have in common? . . . .

What do we need to work on? . . . .

. . . .

9.   *DESIGNING OPTIONS*

What are all the possibilities? *Don't judge them yet. What seems impossible might yield good ideas.*

. . . .

. . . .

. . . .

. . . .

. . . .

Which options give us both more of what we want? *Be creative, mix and match.* . . . .

. . . .

. . . .

10. NEGOTIATION

What do I wish to achieve? *Be really clear about the general outcome, though you may change your route there.* ....
....

How can we make this a fair deal—with both people winning? ....
....

What can they give me? ....
....

What can I give them? ....
....

Am I ignoring objections? Can I include them? ....
....

What points would I want covered in an agreement? ....
....
....
....
....

Is there something that could be included to help them save face? ....
....

Is saving face important to me? Do I particularly need anything? ....

11. MEDIATION

A.   Can we resolve this ourselves or do we need help from a neutral third person? ....
....

Who could take on this role for us? ....
....
....

B. Is mediation the most appropriate role for me in this? If so:

How would I set up and explain my role to both parties? . . . .

. . . .

. . . .

Can I create the right environment for people to open up, understand each other and develop their own solutions? What might help this?

. . . .

. . . .

. . . .

. . . .

12. BROADENING PERSPECTIVES

Am I seeing the whole picture, not just my own point of view? . . . .

What are the effects of this beyond the immediate issue? *(e.g. on other people or groups)* . . . .

. . . .

Where might this lead in the future? . . . .

. . . .

THE RESOLUTION OF CONFLICT

Program notes

Twelve-part audio cassette series

The following notes support an audio cassette series produced by the Australian Broadcasting Corporation. These notes are also useful for group or individual study without the tapes, although playing a tape and then holding a discussion makes an effective session on each skill. This is a convenient teaching format for secondary schools, home study and community groups. Facilitators do not require previous experience in conflict resolution skills, although it is much better to listen to the tape in advance and read the relevant sections in *Everyone Can Win* before the session. Topics are summarised and cross-referenced to supporting material contained in the book.

Key points for consideration are presented as questions. The individual student might jot their own answers down. The questions could also be posed to a group to stimulate discussion before or after playing a tape. It's fine if people offer different answers to the ones on the tape. Just add the missed points after the group contributions. To keep conversation flowing easily in this type of group it's important to ask questions which have no wrong answers. While listening, ask people to make notes on questions or ideas for later discussion. Draw these out at discussion time. Also encourage participants to summarise the main points and to recall experiences that support or contrast with the ideas presented. There are group activity suggestions at the end of each program summary.

Trainers' manuals are readily available through The Conflict Resolution Network for more extensive conflict resolution group facilitation.

Program 1: Win/Win

In this introductory program The Conflict Resolution Network, its origins and purpose are discussed (pp. 7–8). The possibility for better handling conflict in our lives, and using it to sort out difficulties between people are considered. The way we handle conflict makes the difference (p. 9).

Consider: *What are some of the destructive results of conflict that you have experienced? (p. 11)*

Consider: *What positive outcomes have you had from conflict? (p. 12)*

Consider: *What skills do you think you could improve to help you handle conflict more constructively?*

The skills suggested included: • Controlling emotions • Being more logical • Leaving options open • Stress management • Understanding the motivations and reactions of others • Flexibility • Communication skills.

Win/Win: We can often have a co-operative approach where both parties get more of what they want. From the orange story we learn that the first step is to go back to needs. Move away from solutions being proposed and analyse needs. Then work out a way in which each party gets more of what they want (pp. 18–21).

Consider: *How do you react in conflict situations? (pp. 15–18)*

The options suggested included: • Withdrawal • Suppression • Compromise • Win/Lose (as in sport, politics and business). The preferred approach option is Win/Win (pp. 25–6).

Group Activity

The Handshake Game

Ask participants to choose someone to work with, then ask them to stand opposite each other, joining hands in a handshake fashion. Before the game begins, announce the two rules:

1. Win as many points as you can.
2. Each person wins a point when the joined hands touch their hip. Please keep count of your score.

Repeat the rules if necessary, but without explanation. Play the game for up to two minutes. Canvas scores in the group. Discuss the process. How were points won? Which of the approach options were used? Who used the win/win approach with which both people scored lots of points through co-operation?

Program 2: The Creative Response

The last program was about a change in attitude from win/lose to win/win. This program is also about attitude—how to consciously direct a difficult situation toward the positive, and how to open up to possibilities. First we need to understand the developing levels of conflict.

Conflict Clues (pp. 12–14)

Discomfort—little is said but things don't feel right

Incident—mild problems which may not be handled well

Misunderstanding—confusion, poor communication, worry about the difficulties in relating

Tension—'bushfires' break out, perceptions are altered, misinterpretation

Crisis—a relationship breaks up, someone is fired, violence, people may act irrationally

Consider: *Can you remember the first warning signs of discomfort that led to a recent conflict? What could have been said or done at that stage?*

Consider: *Should we try to prevent conflict?*

Perfection-Discovery: Preconceived ideas and demands for perfection from ourselves and others lead to judgmental attitudes and frustration. By contrast, conflict seen as a 'field of enquiry' elicits the creative response and brings a sense of fascination and discovery (pp. 28-31).

Consider: *In what areas of your life do you demand very high standards of yourself or another person?*

Consider: *Would a more relaxed attitude be helpful?*

Turn Crisis Into Opportunity (pp. 31-3)

Consider: *Can you find the valuable possibilities in a currently frustrating situation? What are they?*

Ask 'How would it be if everything worked out well?' To answer this you might structure positive images or sentences of how you want it to be. Life can respond to your thoughts and create things in the way you imagine them. *We* are the magic ingredient for success when we work toward the positive.

Group Activity

Work as a whole group or in pairs.

1. Ask one person to think of one or more situations they find difficult, and then to visualise a positive outcome. They should be encouraged to answer this question in detail: 'How will it be when it all goes well?' The person creating the positive outcome will need to be prompted with questions like 'What can you hear?', 'How do you feel?'. They should be asked about colours, shapes, conversations, what the people are doing, and so on.
2. Brainstorm a long list of limiting and conflict creating words or phrases, e.g. *but, never, can't, don't.* Then ask the group how to make them positive, e.g., *and, haven't so far, it's better if you do* . . . (pp. 33, 78, 161)

Program 3: Empathy

Small talk develops good communication and rapport. It is a tuning-in process, which is the first step toward trust (pp. 44-6).

Consider: *What blocks the flow of empathy between two people?*

Communication Killers: (pp. 38-41) • Domination (threats, orders, criticism, name-calling) • Manipulation (moralising, using 'ought' or 'should', praising or making the other person feel guilty to get what you want) • Denial (reassuring, changing topics, being overly polite, joking, ignoring feelings) • Disempowerment (diagnosing the problem, giving unsought advice, underestimating their own ability to solve their problems).

Consider: *Which communication killers do you use?*

When you receive a communication killer, you could choose *not* to shut down. You may choose to address the poor communication (p. 42).

Consider: *What helps you trust another person?*

People are more trusting when they feel included, acknowledged, equal, accepted for who they are and how they are at the time (p. 43).

Active Listening (pp. 46–7)

Consider: *Listening is a trust-building process. What does a good listener do?*

Do let them know you're interested and have heard what they have said. Stay on the subject. Feed back your understanding of what they are saying.

Don't interrupt, take the conversation back to yourself, try to fix the conversation in any way, or defend yourself at that time.

People communicate at two levels—the facts as they see them, and their feelings about the situation. Paraphrase your understanding of both levels.

When to Active Listen

1. To collect details (p. 48)
2. When the other person has a problem (p. 50)
3. When the other person is angry with you (p. 51)

Active listening doesn't have to be lengthy. Often using one short statement to show understanding of their side is enough to build trust and empathy.

Work on the relationship independently to the problem. Fix empathy breakdowns as part of the resolution process (p. 55).

Group Activity

1. Ask the participants to make up small role plays that include communication killers, and perform them for the group. Ask the group to spot which killers they were using.
2. Working in pairs (you might perhaps include an observer with each pair) participants practise active listening in each of the three types of structures:
   (a) Collecting details (e.g. one partner wants the other to purchase something on their behalf. The listener asks questions to be sure they have all the information.).
   (b) When the other person is upset (one person talks about an upsetting or perturbing situation and the listener paraphrases content and affirms the feelings).
   (c) When the other person is angry with you (one person pretends to be angry with the listener and the listener reflects and acknowledges what is being said without becoming defensive).
      They should role play topics that are real for them. Swap roles often so everyone has a go.
3. Have an extra long break and enjoy some small talk!

Program 4: Appropriate Assertiveness

Stating Your Needs and Rights

Rights come to us by custom and usage. Learn how to state them clearly, without blame, shame or attack.

Consider: *What are the rights you feel justified in asking for?*

The rights discussed included • Being treated with respect • Being listened to and taken seriously • Being able to say 'no' without feeling guilty • Freedom of choice and mobility • Having one's capabilities trusted • The right to information from professionals • Setting personal and professional priorities • Being able to state what hurts • Getting what you pay for.

Passive, Aggressive and Assertive Behaviour

Flight (pp. 58–9)

Consider: *In which areas do you feel you could be more assertive than you are?*

Fight (pp. 56–7)

Consider: *What are the consequences of being aggressive?*

Flow (p. 59)

Consider: *What have you found useful to help a difficult transaction flow smoothly?*

Centring is a body experience that helps flow (pp. 34–5, 84–5). Flow is standing up for your rights in a way that doesn't violate the rights of others. Flow is being able to explain clearly how things are for you.

'I' Statement Formula (pp. 60–7)

The Action: A neutral description of events . . . (objective).

Your Response: How do you feel/what do you do or feel like doing . . . (without blame).

Your Preference: How would you like it to be for you . . . (no demands or expectations).

Consider: *When could you use an 'I' statement?*

Use 'I' statements when you're angry, irritated or if your needs are not being met. An 'I' statement helps you to define what you don't want, work out what you *do* want, and communicate these in a way that doesn't arouse a defensive response.

Mirroring is a process in which each party first uses active listening and then assertiveness. You reflect what you heard the other person say and check for accuracy before you state *your* position. This way you can state your position while staying attuned to the other person.

Group Activity

1. Each group member thinks of a situation in which they could have been more assertive, and then writes an 'I' statement that they might have addressed to the person involved. Participants read out their written efforts in groups of three or around the whole group. The group checks that the statements are 'clean', i.e. objective, without blame, with no demands or expectations, and 'clear', i.e. they address the real issue and say what needs to be said (p. 66).

2. Using the combination of active listening and 'I' statements, set up a mirroring exercise in groups of three. The first person thinks of a difficulty they are presently experiencing with someone. The second person pretends to be the 'problem' person, and the first person plays themselves. The second person will need a short briefing on situation, personality, major priorities and stances in the conflict. The practice session begins with the first person stating their position. The second person paraphrases what they have heard and checks their understanding of it. Then it's their turn to state their position and the first person must active listen before they can reply. Try to stay in the role for at least two or three minutes and make both characters believable. The third person acts as umpire and afterwards leads a discussion clearing up any poor active listening, blaming or demanding.

Program 5: Co-operative Power

Power is expressed in many forms! Nature has it, we have it, organisations and groups have it. Power is neutral: the way it's used makes it constructive or destructive. 'Ultimate power is the ability to produce the results you desire most and create·value for others in the process. Real power is shared, not imposed.' Anthony Robbins (p. 69).

Consider: *In which situations have you seen power being used inappropriately?*

Consider: *When you let people use power over you, on what is that power based? What is their hold over you? In other words, why do you let them win?*

Common Power Bases: (pp. 69–70) • The power of reward • The threat of punishment • Position • Power over the flow of information • Expertise • The value of a continuing good relationship.

These power bases can be used to increase co-operation and effectiveness or they can be used to manipulate for one's own benefit at the expense of others.

Manipulation vs Influence (p. 70)

Consider: *What's the difference between manipulation and influence?*
• Are people free to refuse?
• Do they know what's being asked?
• Are they left free to decide for themselves?

To avoid manipulation: • Consider consequences • Supply information • Explore alternatives

Team Building

Consider: *What strategies help turn a group into a team?*

Strategies suggested included: • Value contributions • Set goals and rules together • Share information • Be flexible to requests for change • Delegate tasks and responsibility • Give permission to make mistakes.

Personal Power (p. 77)

Consider: *What qualities of personal power do you admire in others?*

Consider: *Are these qualities you would like to develop in yourself to become more powerful?*

Consider:*In which ways do you give your power away? (pp. 78–81)*

Power Triangle (pp. 71–5)

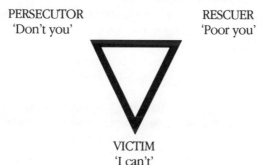

PERSECUTOR   RESCUER
'Don't you'   'Poor you'

VICTIM
'I can't'

Consider: *Does this power structure operate anywhere in your life? Which roles do you play where?*

'I Should' vs 'I Choose' (pp. 78–81)

Consider: *What's the difference for you between these two statements?*

Group Activity

1. As a group, make a list of statements beginning with 'I should . . .' Each person contributes

examples of personal 'shoulds'. Go through the list and upgrade these statements to begin 'I choose . . .' or 'I could . . .'
2. Divide the group into threes. Choose who will play mother, father and child, as illustrated. These roles do not rotate. What does rotate are the Persecutor, Rescuer or Victim positions. Each character uses each position once for three minutes at a time (9 minutes total).

MOTHER
(begin as Persecutor)

FATHER
(begin as Rescuer)

SON/DAUGHTER
(begin as Victim)

Play out a family argument about where to go on holiday. Have a minute of silence between each three-minute session, and ask the participants to note down: a) how they felt using that style and b) what strategies they used to get their way.

When the session is complete, draw out the information on feelings and strategies.

Program 6: Managing Emotions

For most people, emotion is the first sign that discussion has become conflict. Resolution is blocked if the emotions are not handled well. Strong negative emotions can point to the need for change (p. 89).
Consider: *Which emotions do you experience regularly?*
Consider: *What options do you have when you experience a high emotion?*
• **Expression**—telling and demonstrating to the other person exactly how you feel (p. 98).
• **Containment**—acknowledging the feeling and being aware of it until it shifts (pp. 92–8).
• **Suppression**—not letting yourself be aware of the emotion. Emotion is a physical experience. If we suppress it, as many do, it will be stored in the body and affect our health and happiness (pp. 89–90).
• **Release**—discharging the energy into alternative activities (pp. 91–2).
Consider: *How do you choose to release highly charged negative emotions?*
Suggestions included: • Sport and exercise • Drawing • Music • Dancing • Using a punching bag, mattress or pillow • Having a good yell out of earshot • Taking some time out • Walking.
Consider: *How can you contain an emotion without suppressing it?*
Centring is useful, here (p. 84). Take a couple of minutes to bring your attention to your navel area and allow your breathing to deepen so that it moves that area rhythmically. Look for the settling effect. Acknowledge what you are feeling.
Questions and Goals: Now that your emotion has been acknowledged and released, or contained through centring, how can you work with it toward resolution of the conflict? Next time you're upset, ask yourself the following questions: (pp. 98–9) • Why am I feeling this emotion? • What do I want to change? • What do I need in order to release this emotion? • Who

has the problem? Which part of the problem is mine and which part is theirs? • What is the unspoken message I interpret from this situation? (e.g. 'She thinks she's better than me.')

If you choose to express how you are feeling to the other person, try to achieve the following goals: • Communicate your feelings—without threat or punishment • Change the situation • Prevent the same problem recurring • Increase communication and improve the relationship.

When people are prepared to share their emotions with each other, there is real depth to the relationship. Therefore, other people's emotions need to be acknowledged by us—not denied or dampened (p. 100).

People who are highly emotional need support and some reassurance, even if you are the object of their anger. You may need to recognise their hidden motive. The need for attention, power, revenge or fear of inadequacy may lie beneath difficult behaviour in others (pp. 100–101).

Group Activity

1. Have each person think of a recent, unpleasant emotional event. Spend several minutes writing answers to the exercise on pp. 102–103. In pairs discuss the difficulties and any insights.
2. Some groups might enjoy taking turns to mime how they feel right now while the rest of the participants guess the emotion. This increases the available vocabulary of 'emotion' words.

Program 7: Willingness to Resolve

Anger, resentment and revenge contribute to the inhibition of successful conflict resolution (p. 104).

Consider: *Why are these emotions hard to shift? (pp. 104–106)*

These emotions are often sustained by the reservoir of unresolved material hidden in the subconscious mind. Carl Jung called this material the 'Shadow'. It is the part of ourselves we deny. Qualities we find unacceptable in ourselves we project onto another person or group. The unconscious has a strong influence over our negative and more irrational reactions. Much of our capacity for joy and creativity can also be suppressed and bound up in the Shadow (pp. 108–109).

Informed or Inflamed? (pp. 107–108)

Consider: *How can we recognise when Shadow material is influencing our willingness to resolve?*

Clue: When a situation *informs* us, then all is well. You only have the problem itself to sort out. When it *inflames* us, some projection is going on as well.

Consider: *What sort of material is stored in the unconscious? (pp. 110–111)*

• Suppressed needs
• Unresolved personal history
• Unacceptable negative qualities

When you blame the other person for your own unacknowledged issues you feel justified and righteous about your position, which can stand in the way of your willingness to resolve.

Jung said when something is not acknowledged consciously, it manifests itself as fate. It may continue to recur until we acknowledge it, i.e. bring the suppressed understanding or feeling into consciousness.

Examples:

Suppressed need: A woman feels angry when someone wolf-whistles at her. She realises that underneath her anger she feels threatened, and had not really acknowledged her need to be safe and secure.

Unresolved personal history: A man wasn't allowed to keep his teenage treasures. He had not acknowledged how angry he was about it, and now feels resentful about his own child's 'hoarding'.

Unacceptable negative qualities: Long and deeply repressed terror may cause irrational violence. Sometimes remembering alone is not enough to change things, and similar situations keep on presenting themselves. We may need to play out the new situation more successfully than the old. In this way, we redesign the patterns of the past. We may need to forgive in order to release ourselves from the problem (pp. 112–113).

When the other person is unwilling to resolve, look at anything you might be doing that could be contributing to their defensiveness or resentment (pp. 114–15).

Group Activity

1. If members of your group would like to find out more about why they react the way they do, take some time in the group to do the exercise on p. 112 privately on paper. Debrief the group as seems appropriate, and in pairs. What questions are raised by the exercise? What have participants learned?
2. You can follow this exercise with another pen and paper exercise, asking this question, 'Who do you need to forgive?' Ask the participants to address that person mentally in completing the following sentences:

- I forgive you for . . .
- I ask your forgiveness for . . .
- I forgive myself for . . . in relation to this difficulty.

Be aware that participants may have explored their feelings deeply in these two exercises. Allow time to debrief. Use active listening to acknowledge insights. Being heard is very healing. It is usually not necessary or appropriate to do more than this in this type of group.

Program 8: Mapping the Conflict

Consider: *Why is a map useful? (p. 117)*
Responses include: • To help us get from where we are to where we want to go • To show things in relation to each other • To show where there are obstacles in the way • To show which directions are easiest to take • To show difficulties we may have to deal with • To show our choices.

When we map a conflict situation we use the map for these same reasons: to find out all possible information and all the feelings involved, and then to use this clarification to discover our options and plan actions.

Mapping Needs and Fears

What is the problem about? Name it briefly. Write this title at the centre of your sheet of paper (p. 117). Then, spaced around the outside of the sheet, write down the participants or the groups affected by the outcome (p. 118). For each of these people or groups, ask the following two questions and list the answers:

What are the needs here? Needs may be both material and emotional, and include values and preferences (pp. 120–1).

What are the fears here? Fears may include anxieties and things we wouldn't want to happen (p. 120).

In mapping the needs and fears for each party, you will discover a lot about underlying motivations (p. 121).

You can follow how this map was made as you listen to the program.

ABORIGINAL TEACHERS	NON-ABORIGINAL TEACHERS
Needs:	**Needs:**
• Income	• To meet educational and classroom requirements
• Recognition	• To be regarded as a professional
• To make a contribution	• To maintain status
• Job satisfaction	
Fears:	**Fears:**
• Unemployment	• Being seen to be insensitive to Aboriginal issues
• Seen to be of little or no value	• Qualifications, recognition and status could be devalued
• Their value could be usurped by non-Aboriginal people	• Loss of credibility

WHO TEACHES ABORIGINAL STUDIES

EDUCATION DEPARTMENT
Needs:
• An effective program
• To define qualifications
• To meet the needs of Aboriginal students
Fears:
• Loss of validity
• Alienating Aboriginal students
• Taking an anthropological approach rather than life experience

Consider: *How did the mapping exercise help the participants? (pp. 123–5)*
Did you notice: • How much the parties involved had in common? • That the attitudes that emerge shift as each side is validated, and hears the other side's point of view? • The clarity that emerges as the needs and fears are revealed and analysed?
Mapping makes the issues clear, stops the blame, and points the way to options (p. 125).

Group Activity
Ask for volunteers who would be willing to have a conflict mapped by the group. It should be current and unresolved. Consider several alternatives. Ask the group to vote for which map they'd like to concentrate on.

Adapt the format used on p. 118 to plot the parties involved and list the needs and fears for each. Analyse your map by looking for the common ground. Brainstorm some options. Program 9 will provide many more suggestions for developing options out of a map.

Program 9: Development of Options

Design New Choices: If someone is dissatisfied with the solution then the resolution is not complete. We need to search for positive solutions that work for everyone, and we need to be practical and realistic in our hunt for solutions (pp. 130-1).
Consider: *How would you test the effectiveness of a solution? (pp. 135-6)*
• Is it enough, i.e. sufficient to satisfy everyone's needs?
• Is it feasible?
• Is it operational, i.e. Can we do it? Will it work?

Creativity: (pp. 130-1) Win/win solutions will challenge your creativity and ingenuity. To start the ball rolling, be sure you're defining the problem in terms of needs, not in terms of solutions. Preconceived ideas about the solution will limit the process of developing options. Often we're not very clear about what it is exactly that we need—it's often easier to know what we *don't* want. Roll the negatives through to their positive counterparts. Knowing what you don't want may help you come up with what you do want instead.

Brainstorming:
Consider: *What are some useful rules for brainstorming? (p. 132)*
For a limited period of time write down every idea that comes. Don't edit, censor, evaluate or comment on ideas.

Chunking: (pp. 133-4) Is the problem too complex? Chunk it! Break it down into smaller, more manageable units and work on it piece by piece. By using a chunking process, a number of very practical options arose from the issue mapped in the last program.

Designing: When designing solutions, consider what underlying question the various participants feel they are being asked. Are there misconceptions? What are the consequences of the suggested solutions? Are there any objective standards of fairness that can be used to evaluate solutions? (p. 136) Elegant solutions are of low cost to one party and of high value to another. Such solutions are very inviting (see Currencies on pp. 132-3).
Consider: *What can you do if the other person refuses to co-operate in the search for better solutions? (p. 135)*
You may need to confront them with the consequences of non-co-operation.
Consider: *What can you do if solutions won't come? (p. 133)*
It will probably be useful to collect more information. Decide what information you need and where you will get it from (p. 131).

Group Activity
Develop the options that were discovered in your group mapping exercise in the last session or make a new map and develop new options, bearing the following points in mind: • Be clear about needs • Clarify misconceptions • Brainstorm possibilities • Are there objective standards of fairness? • Is chunking appropriate here? • Are there elements that could be traded which are valuable to one party and easy for the other to give? • Do you need more information? • What information? • Where could you get it?

Program 10: Negotiation

Negotiation skills will help you to build a suitable environment for working toward a win/win resolution. Formally or informally, we negotiate every day. A negotiation gathers the parties together to fulfill their various needs (pp. 138-9).

Preparation

Consider: *How can you prepare yourself for a negotiation? (p. 139)*

Some suggested preparations: • Map out the needs and fears—yours, theirs and any other relevant group • Collect information—as much as you can find • Develop some options • Establish a good relationship, if possible, prior to the negotiation proper.

Win/Win tactics during negotiation:

Consider: *What strategies and techniques have you found valuable during negotiations? Which strategies particularly help a win/win approach? (pp. 140-1)*

Some suggested strategies and techniques: • Establish rapport early • Discuss the issues broadly • Emphasise 'common ground', what have you in common? (p. 140) • Be willing to talk things through • Be open to a wide range of possibilities • Find out what lies behind their demands. Often a conflict is presented as a set of proposed solutions. Is there another way to solve the conflict? • Maintain a good relationship • Be soft on the person and hard on the problem (p. 143) • Use 'and' not 'but' to include objections (p. 144) • Be aware of the influence of those not present.

Consider: *What hinders win/win negotiating?*

Negotiate fairly. Don't win over the other person just because you can. Don't go along with an agreement just to be agreeable.

The Close

Consider: *What should you be doing at the end of a negotiation? (p. 148)*

Suggested closing considerations: • Create contracts or clear agreements • Establish a checking system to be sure your agreement will not break down • Make sure the other parties 'save face' and 'look good' at the end • Invest in the ongoing relationship • Create a balanced deal. All parties need to feel good about the deal for it to work.

Countertactics

Consider: *What can you do when the other person is using win/lose tactics against you? (pp. 146-7)*

Some suggestions: • If they are being rude, ignore it, and acknowledge their legitimate concerns. • Ask a question. • Restate it in more neutral terms. • Write things down. • Call a break—take time out.

Group Activity

Ask the group to propose negotiation situations that are relevant and simple. Choose one to work with.

1. Ask the group to prepare for the negotiation by mapping it.
2. Invite a number of pairs to go through the negotiation in front of the group. One person may be asked to play a very difficult character to negotiate with. Discuss the different styles and consider how the participants might handle obstructive behaviour.

Program 11: Mediation

When good communication has broken down, calling in a third party mediator is a responsible way to proceed. Taking a dispute to litigation requires the surrender of decision-making power to a higher authority. Many issues between people do not require, or would not be appropriate in a courtroom process (pp. 150-1).

A number of schools in Australia and elsewhere have taught mediation and installed mediation structures. It is very beneficial during peer conflicts, and helps to reduce discipline problems in schools. Mediation has been taught to students from as young as seven years of age through to teenagers (p. 152).

Conflict resolution skills in mediation: (pp. 155-9) The techniques of mediation are natural extensions of conflict resolution skills. Active listening, empathy, mapping and brainstorming are often employed in the process. Good conflict resolvers can become mediators—at work and at home. Mediating is often done very informally in discussion (pp. 153-4). Grievance handling in the workplace may be approached informally though sometimes a special officer and formal procedures will be needed (p. 155).

Roles
Consider: *If you needed a mediator how would you like them to be?*
Their role is to help the parties involved in the dispute to talk about the issues in a constructive and productive way, which will help them to reach agreement. The mediator aims to help both parties get what they need. The mediator should be objective, empathic and non-judgmental (pp. 150, 157).
Consider: *What ground rules and guidelines did you notice the mediator in this program following? (pp. 157-63)*
Recognisable ground rules and guidelines: • Lead participants away from shaming, blaming or attacking (p. 161) • Help them to be sure that they really want to see the problem fixed (p. 158) • Encourage them to listen to each other by checking back • Validate each point of view (p. 162) • Find out what was really going on for each person • Get them to talk about their feelings • Help them to make 'I' statements—to explain how it was for them, rather than what the other person should do (p. 158) • Include all views in solution-hunting • Seek co-operation in the development of agreements • Find out what they would do if the agreement broke down (p. 163).
Remember: A good mediator teaches conflict resolution skills along the way to resolution.

Group Activity
Find a simple and familiar conflict situation. By working in small groups, role play a mediation sequence. Try out a variety of mediation skills. For example, one group could map the conflict. Another could have a session of conducted active listening, with the mediator directing the process. A third could work with the mediator to make clean 'I' statements to each other about the problem. Another could work with the creative response, finding the value in the situation and creating images of 'how it will be when it all goes well', and so on.

Program 12: Broadening Perspectives

Many viewing points: With a broader perspective we can recognise that we see things subjectively, and need to look at things from different points of view. We recognise that the other points of view are necessary and valid parts of the whole picture (p. 165).
Consider: *Why do people resist taking a broader perspective?*
The skill is often difficult to apply when there is a fear of losing your own ground if you really listen to other people's points of view.

The need for a broader view applies at the interpersonal as well as the international level of conflict (pp. 165-9). Here we consider Broadening Perspectives in a number of specific major problem areas. The political will to build a co-operative world depends on the consideration of many factors including economic and ecological ones. We can all participate in the peace process by practising good conflict resolution skills in schools, legal systems and in the media. The cultural consequences of constructive conflict resolution could mean a more equitable society in which more people have more of their needs met.

Consider: *We are all part of the one system. What are the implications of this?*

The broader perspective shows that we can all make a difference to bring peace to our own lives, our society, our nation and our planet. As we climb higher up the mountain of understanding ourselves and others, we find a broader view (pp. 169–70).

Group Activity

Ask the group to suggest some specific current conflicts at community, national or international levels. Use group discussion to develop a broader view of each of these topics. How can this broader view make a difference in the constructive resolution of these situations? Will your group commit to some action that will make a difference?

Take your skills out into the world!

Index